philosophia naturalis

Journal for the Philosophy of Nature

49 / 2012 / 1

Herausgeber / Editors
Andreas Bartels
Bernd-Olaf Küppers
C. Ulises Moulines

Beirat / Editorial Board
Werner Diederich (Hamburg)
Michael Esfeld (Lausanne)
Don Howard (Notre Dame)
Andreas Hüttemann (Münster)
Bernulf Kanitscheider (Gießen)
Daryn Lehoux (Kingston, Ontario)
James Lennox (Pittsburgh)
Holger Lyre (Magdeburg)
Peter Mittelstaedt (Köln)
Felix Mühlhölzer (Göttingen)
Friedrich Rapp (Dortmund)
Friedrich Steinle (Berlin)
Manfred Stöckler (Bremen)
Eckart Voland (Gießen)
Gerhard Vollmer (Braunschweig)
Marcel Weber (Konstanz)
Michael Wolff (Bielefeld)

KLOSTERMANN

Cord Friebe (ed.) TEMPORAL EXISTENCE AND PERSISTENCE IN SPACETIME

The articles are indexed in *The Philosopher's Index* and *Mathematical Reviews.*

Abonnenten der Printausgabe können über Ingentaconnect auf die Online-Ausgabe der Zeitschrift zugreifen: *www.ingentaconnect.com*

Zurückliegende Jahrgänge sind mit einer Sperrfrist von fünf Jahren für die Abonnenten von *www.digizeitschriften.de* zugänglich.

© Vittorio Klostermann GmbH, Frankfurt am Main 2012

Die Zeitschrift und alle in ihr enthaltenen Beiträge und Abbildungen sind urheberrechlich geschützt. Jede Verwertung außerhalb der Grenzen des Urheberrechtsgesetzes ist ohne Zustimmung des Verlages unzulässig. Das gilt insbesondere für Vervielfältigungen, Übersetzungen, Mikroverfilmungen und Einspeicherung und Verarbeitung in elektronischen Systemen.

Satz: Mirjam Loch, Frankfurt am Main / Druck: KM-Druck, Groß-Umstadt.
Gedruckt auf alterungsbeständigem Papier ∞ ISO 9706.

ISBN 978-3-465-04155-9
ISSN 0031-8027

Preface

Relativity still challenges the philosophy of time: although several sophisticated theories of temporal existence and persistence have been developed in the last decades, there is still an ongoing debate about how to apply the various concepts to spacetime theories and about whether those distinctions are even relevant at all for the ontology of spacetime. As it turns out ontologists of spacetime physics can broadly be arranged into two different camps: the first group is concerned with the apparently central question in the philosophy of (space-)time, i.e., whether the present is ontologically distinguished. The second deals with the problem of temporal change: material objects persist through (space-) time and survive change – how do they manage to do so? Both debates have reached a high level of specialization; they are 'overspecialized', in my view, and need to be interrelated. So, the main purpose of this issue is: to bring together "temporal existence" and "persistence" in spacetime. I shall say in few words about why this is a desideratum and why this could be fruitful.

Since the famous Putnam/Stein-controversy (1967/68) philosophers of spacetime physics have examined the relation between *time* and *reality*. Is the present ontologically distinguished – or by being the edge of determination (growing block view), separating an 'open' future from a 'fixed' past, or even existentially by being *all* there is (presentism)? Or, is spacetime rather, somehow, a 'static' block universe within all events exist simply by being located somewhere, at some spacetime point p or other, independently of p being present? And, if so, is there any room in that block universe for *becoming* (as opposed to merely being) and for *change* (as opposed to mere spatial variation)? All these questions are usually discussed under the common assumption that the fundamental entities in spacetime are *point-events*, i.e., spatially and temporally unextended simples – Einsteinian flashes of lightning, for example. *Compositions* of those point-events into spatially extended wholes or into temporally extended objects have been considered, for a long time, as being merely pragmatic. Persistence as a matter of ontology was – in its application to spacetime theories – for many years not considered. But this seems to be idiosyncratic, in my view. Firstly, from a historical point of view: According to Kant, to give a paradigmatic example and to mention a classical presentist (at least as I would read him), "Beharrlichkeit" is the criterion of "Wirklichkeit", thus persistence is essential for temporal existence. Secondly, from a purely analytical standpoint: According to Mellor, to mention a paradigmatic contemporary eternalist, persistence (endurance, in this case) is likewise essential for temporal existence, namely in order to give "existence" a temporal content, in particular, to distinguish temporal change from a-temporal variation. Hence, the temporal-existence group should say more about persistence.

On the other hand, the ontology of persistence and change – namely, in terms of contemporary analytic philosophy, the investigation of whether objects survive change by being "wholly present" at more than one time (endurantism) or by having different "temporal parts" (perdurantism) – has been discussed so far, by philosophers of spacetime physics, *exclusively* with the underlying assumption of the so-called eternalist hypothesis. But this is apparently too restrictive: it firstly suggests (wrongly, in my view) that other views of time and reality are already refuted by the theories of relativity. Why not consider, for instance, persisting objects in a growing block universe? At least in the light of quantum physics, relativity should be compatible with an ontological *indeterminism* and so, perhaps, with a *dynamic* view of temporal existence. Several interesting questions concerning persisting objects may arise: what does it mean, for example, that a persisting object *perdures* if the world is dynamical and/or indeterministic? Secondly, the underlying eternalist hypothesis itself seems to be *ambiguous*: Sometimes the block universe is conceived of in a way that does *not* allow for any (objective) temporally restricted or 'perspectival' sense of "existence". And sometimes, in contrast, there *is* distinguished a narrow concept of "existence-at" from an unrestricted "existence-*simpliciter*". So, it threatens a switching between two different block universe views, with important consequences for the endurance/perdurance distinction. The eternalist hypothesis should therefore be reconsidered, and the persistence-camp should also broaden its scope.

This special issue collects papers from the international workshop entitled "Temporal Existence and Persistence in Spacetime" which was held at the University Club Bonn, in February 2011. Many thanks to all the speakers and participants for stimulating talks and fruitful discussions – in particular I would like to thank Natalja Deng, Friedrich Karl Kraemer, Thomas Müller (Lausanne), Paul M. Näger, Geurt Sengers, Rainer Stuhlmann-Laeisz, Antonio Vassallo, Emanuel Viebahn, Sandra Völler, and Daniel Wohlfarth. For his effective organizational assistance I am deeply grateful to Christopher Pierog, and, for the poster-design, to Andrea Wille and Peter Steffens. Special thanks to DFG and GAP for their financial support. Finally, I would like to thank Andreas Bartels, the chair of the philosophy of science group at Bonn University, and Carsten Seck, for managing the journal affairs.

Cord Friebe, Saarbrücken, February 2012

Yuri Balashov

Do Composite Objects Have an Age in Relativistic Spacetime?

Abstract

Momentary locations of point-size objects in Minkowski spacetime can be usefully labeled by their proper time – the invariant time measured along their trajectories. There is a good sense in which proper time can represent the age of such an object (if the object has a finite age). But is there a well-defined notion of age for composite objects consisting of many particles in complex relative motion? Relatedly, what could serve as a measure of proper time for such an object? And is there a good procedure for its determination? Surprisingly, the issue has rarely been discussed. I attempt to remedy that situation and offer some comments.

Zusammenfassung

Momentane Positionen punktartiger Objekte in Minkowskis Raumzeit können durch deren Eigenzeit – die invariante, längs ihrer Weltlinien gemessenen Zeit – brauchbar gekennzeichnet werden. Es gibt einen guten Sinn, in dem Eigenzeit das Alter eines solchen Objektes repräsentieren kann (insofern das Objekt ein begrenztes Alter hat). Doch gibt es einen wohldefinierten Begriff des Alters auch für zusammengesetzte Systeme, die aus vielen Teilchen bestehen, die in beliebiger relativer Bewegung sein können? Was kann entsprechend als Maß der Eigenzeit für ein solches Objekt dienen? Und gibt es ein gutes Verfahren, sie zu bestimmen? Überraschenderweise sind diese Fragen bislang nur selten diskutiert worden. Ich versuche, diesen Mangel zu beheben, und gebe ein paar Kommentare.

1. Introduction

Many material objects come to be and cease to exist. It is customary to speak of their age. In the classical spacetime framework, the age of an object can be used to label its momentary locations – three-dimensional slices of a four-dimensional path in spacetime. This comes in handy in some metaphysical discussions, such as the debate about persistence.[1]

The situation becomes more complex in the framework of relativity. In Minkowski spacetime, momentary locations of *non-extended* point-like objects can certainly be tracked, labeled or indexed with their *proper time* – the invariant time τ measured along their trajectories:

$$\tau = \int \frac{dt}{\gamma} = \int \sqrt{1 - \frac{v(t)^2}{c^2}} dt \tag{1a}$$

$$\tau = \int \sqrt{\left(\frac{dt}{ds}\right)^2 - \frac{1}{c^2}\left(\left(\frac{dx}{ds}\right)^2 + \left(\frac{dy}{ds}\right)^2 + \left(\frac{dx}{ds}\right)^2\right)} ds \tag{1b}$$

$$\tau = \int_L \sqrt{dt^2 - \frac{dx^2}{c^2} - \frac{dy^2}{c^2} - \frac{dz^2}{c^2}} \tag{1c}$$

(1a) and (1b) are calculated in a given Cartesian coordinate system (t, x, y, z), and s is a real-valued parameter that can be used to define a spacetime trajectory or path of a material point: $t = t(s)$, $x = x(s)$, $y = y(s)$, and $z = z(s)$. Alternatively, τ can be calculated in terms of a line integral along the object's path L, as in (1c). There is a good sense in which τ can represent the age of such an object (if the object has a finite age).

But what about composite objects consisting, say, of many particles in complex relative motion? Is there a well-defined notion of age for them? And for that matter, is there a well-defined notion of proper time for them? Even if we restrict instantaneous locations of such objects to flat spacelike hypersurfaces[2] they will, in general, "crisscross," even within the object's path, and it is not immediately obvious how one is supposed to identify, label or order them. More precise outlines of the problem will emerge shortly. Here I hasten to note that although in many situations one can simply abstract from the size and composite nature of material objects and continue to work with point idealizations, sooner or later the issue needs to be discussed. And there may be independent interest, both physical and philosophical, in raising it. It is interesting to know whether the notion of age can be coherently applied to composite objects in Minkowski or general relativistic spacetime, and if so, whether there is a good procedure for its determination. Surprisingly, the issue has rarely been discussed. Below I attempt to remedy that situation and offer some comments.

2. Tangential Worries: Metaphysics of Composition

Do composite materials objects have an age? Raising this question may bring with it some interesting and famous, but tangential problems having to do with the metaphysics of composition, which I would like to set aside here. In this particular case, the worry boils down to the question of when a given composite object comes into existence. What defines the beginning of its career and a zero point from which we could start tracking its age? Suppose we have n sufficiently scattered particles that come together to compose object o. When exactly does it happen? And how can we be sure that o maintains its existence later on? Important as these questions may be there is nothing particularly relativistic about them, and they are logically independent of the issues I wish to discuss here.

Accordingly, I will simply assume that these more metaphysical concerns can be put to rest and we can focus on other important questions. In fact, the underlying situation I would like to presuppose is a situation in which a certain composite object starts its career at a certain moment of time t_0 in a certain frame of reference (Figure 1) and never goes out of existence. The particles composing it pursue their separate trajectories in Minkowski spacetime. The interesting question then is: how can we track the career of the whole object and measure its age?

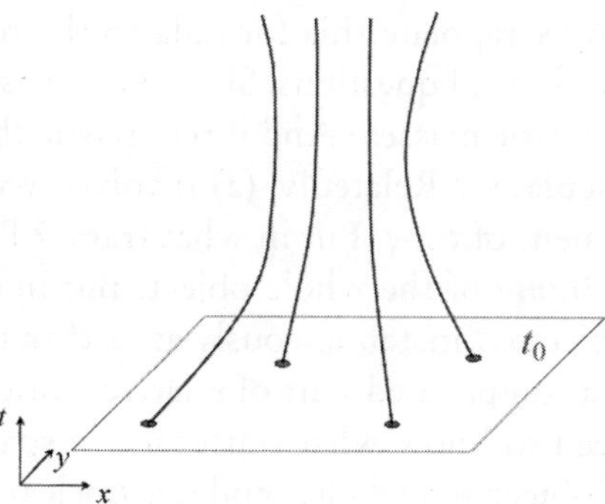

Figure 1. A composite object comes into existence at t_0 in (t, x, y, z).

3. It's Not Easy!

Initially one might think that the task should be relatively easy. After all, we have all these particles and their proper times (Eqs. 1a–1c); so one might hope that, somehow or other, they would "average out." Perhaps we can take an initial clue from a classical case, where it is natural and trivial to associate the spacetime trajectory of a composite object *o* with the trajectory of its *center of mass* (the bold line in Figure 2):

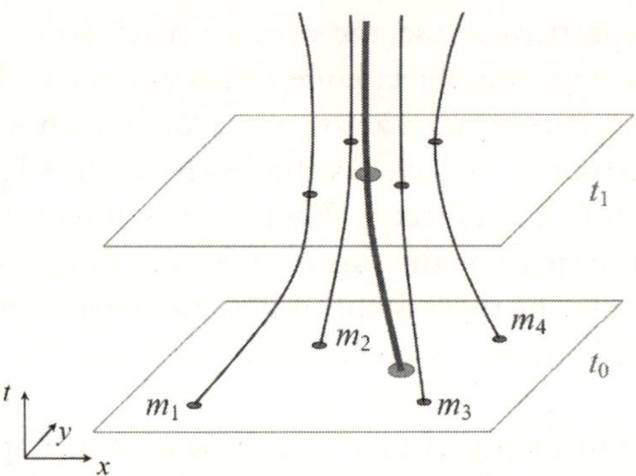

Figure 2. Spacetime trajectory of the center of mass of a composite object in classical spacetime.

where the radius vector of the center of mass $\mathbf{r}_o$ at any given moment of time is simply the weighted sum of the radius vectors of the components:

$$\mathbf{r}_o = \Sigma m_i \mathbf{r}_i \,/\, \Sigma m_i \tag{2}$$

But any attempt to extrapolate this formula to the relativistic context immediately raises a host of questions. Should the masses in question be rest masses or relativistic masses? And if relativistic then in what frame should they be calculated? Relatedly, (2) involves 3-vectors and refers to a particular moment of time. But in what frame? Presumably, in the *instantaneous rest frame* of the whole object. But in order to know in which frame the object is "instantaneously at rest" in the case of *n* constituent particles in a complicated state of relative motion it would appear that we already need to know what trajectory in spacetime represents the motion of the "object as a whole," and it is unclear that this could be known without knowing the trajectory of the object's center of mass.

We seem to be in a circle. In addition, we cannot simply assume, as we do in classical mechanics, that the frame in which the object as a whole is at rest must automatically coincide with the frame in which the total momentum is zero. We can *decide* that this should be the case. Natural though it may seem, it would be a substantive decision.

One still hopes that there should be a reasonably straightforward way out of this circular mess. This hope, however, is dashed rather dramatically by considering a case of an object (Gibson and Pooley, 2006, 194, note 29) composed of two oscillating point particles of equal mass, moving uniformly towards and away from each other at the same speed (Figure 3a) in frame (x,t). Obviously the object as a whole is at rest at any moment in this frame: at t_1, t_2, t_3, etc. But it is *also* periodically at rest in a different frame (x',t') co-moving with one of the particles: e.g., at t_1' and t_2'. So the object is at rest in *both* frames that are in relative motion!

This shows that the instantaneous rest frame of a composite object is not an easily-defined concept. Note that this is shown *independently* of evaluating the prospects of any candidate for the role of the center of mass. And when it comes to the latter, the symmetry line of the diagram (Figure 3b) is an obvious candidate for the trajectory of the center of mass of the composite object. But a line that would include the oblique fragments plus some fragments of the symmetry line would also be a good candidate.

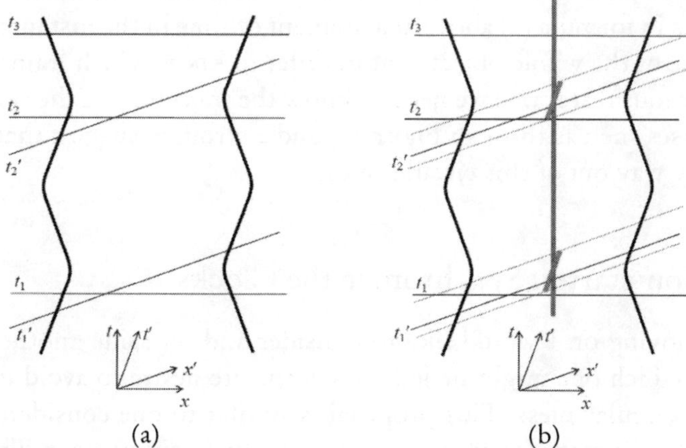

Figure 3. A composite object is at rest in two different frames of reference.

Another curious, even if less realistic, case[3] includes an object composed of a linear array of *infinitely* many identical point particles, each receding from its neighbor at the same relative velocity v. The spacetime trajectory of *any* such particle – or, for that matter, of any symmetry line of this configuration – could be taken to represent, equally well, the trajectory of the whole object – an extreme case in point (Figure 4)! Below I abstract from such examples involving an infinite number of material parts and focus on a system of n particles.

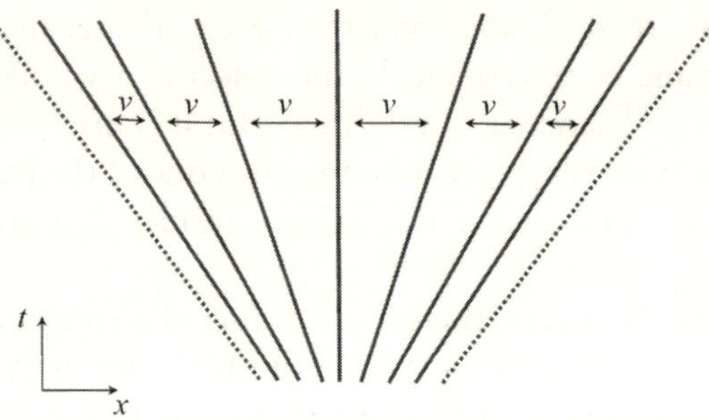

Figure 4. An object composed of an infinite number of mutually receding particles is at rest in an infinite number of reference frames.

Is there *any* general way to define a unique trajectory representing, somehow or other, the motion of an arbitrary composite object in Minkowski spacetime? To sum up the problem so far, in order to determine the trajectory of the center of mass we need to calculate all the quantities in formula (2) above at a moment of time in the instantaneous rest frame of the whole object. But in order to know which frame is the instantaneous rest frame we need to know the trajectory of the center of mass. Cases such as those in Figures 3 and 4 strongly suggest that there is no easy way out of this circular mess.

4. A Non-starter: Synchronize the Clocks

Before moving on I would like to consider and set aside another proposal to which one might be led by a desperate desire to avoid dealing with the circular mess. This proposal is similar to one considered and rejected by Gilmore (2008, 1239–1240) in a different context. The idea is to attach a small clock to each particle, set them all to zero at t_0, then track the proper time of each particle with its corresponding clock, and then simply mark the locations of all the particles after 1 second, after 2 seconds, etc. of their proper times. Once we have these locations we can draw hypersurfaces through them and identify the resulting filled regions with the locations of the whole object at the age of 1 second, at the age of 2 seconds, etc. (Figure 5). And once we have such locations we can, if we wish, determine the position of the center of mass at each of them and then connect them, thereby producing a spacetime trajectory of the whole object.

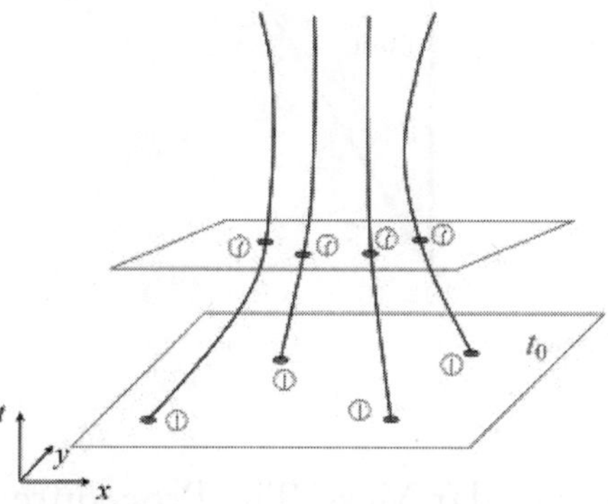

Figure 5. Synchronize the clocks!

This proposal is untenable because the resulting regions defined according to its prescription will quickly go wild. At some point they will stop being spacelike and even sooner they will stop being flat. This is easy to see if we help ourselves to a small "twins scenario." Call one particle Alice and another Bob (Figure 6). Alice comes back to reunite with Bob, and continues to stay with him, and she is so much younger. So if we wanted to synchronize their ages in the way suggested we would need to put the 20-year old Alice at a point timelike separated from the location of the 20-year old Bob. When considered at these two locations, Alice and Bob cannot compose anything worthwhile.

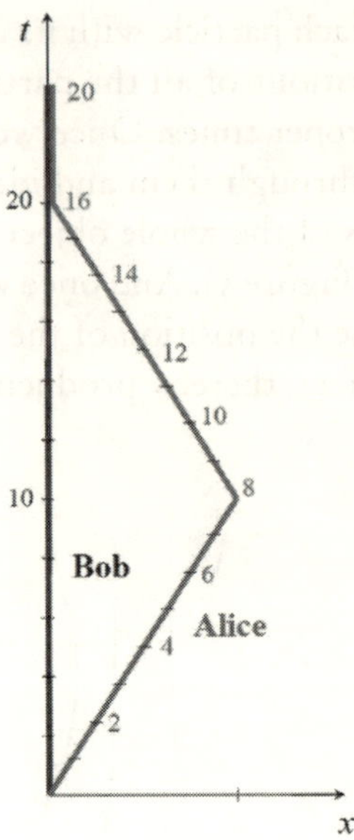

Figure 6. Alice and Bob.

5. Back to the Circular Mess: The Procedure

So we do need to deal with the circular mess. Is there *any* general way to define a trajectory representing, somehow or other, the motion of an arbitrary composite object in Minkowski spacetime? One would expect there to be some history of the discussion of this question and some authoritative work. And there is; but it is scanty.[4] Pryce (1948) and Schattner (1978; 1979), in particular, are frequently cited in later developments.[5] The interest in the problem seems to have been driven by rather diverse motivations ranging from predominantly mathematical curiosity to attempts to use the resulting constructions as a bridge between the micro and the macro to draw some rough-and-ready consequences for the foundations of quantum physics.[6] The exact details of the more serious developments lie beyond my mathematical expertise. But I wish to note a convergence of some of these developments with my own ideas, to which I was led before becoming aware of this larger literature (Balashov, 2010, 191–195). Accordingly, I will take the liberty to sketch my toy procedure to determine the worldline of an arbitrary object composed of n non-interacting particles, in Minkowski spacetime. It is far from rigorous and has other limitations too. But it will allow me to illustrate the basic idea in simple terms. I discuss the limitations and necessary refinements in section 6.

The basic idea, in the idealized case of n non-interacting particles, is to chart the trajectory of a composite object by connecting the locations of its center of mass determined in instantaneous frames in which the total momentum is zero, using relativistic quantities (i.e. dynamic masses, etc.), and then translate the result to an arbitrary frame by a Lorentz transformation. This is then how the circle could be broken – by identifying the zero-momentum frame first.

In a bit more detail:[7] consider object o composed of n particles o_1, o_2, ... o_n with continuous and smooth trajectories $\mathbf{r}_i = \mathbf{r}_i(s)$, $t = t(s)$ in a coordinate system $(\mathbf{r},t)$ adapted to some inertial reference frame, where s is a real-valued parameter. We are looking for a trajectory $\mathbf{r}_o = \mathbf{r}_o(s)$, $t_o = t_o(s)$ representing (somehow or other) the motion of o. Choose some particle o_1 and its location $(\mathbf{r}_1(s),t(s))$, for some value of s. The most important step then is to identify a time hyperplane through $(\mathbf{r}_1(s),t(s))$, at which the total 3-momentum of o is zero. That is to say, we should identify a reference frame F(s) (an "instantaneous rest frame of o") such that, for some coordinate system $(\mathbf{r}^F,t^F)$ adapted to F, a particular time hyperplane $t^F=t^F(s)$ contains $(\mathbf{r}_1(s),t(s))$ and $|\Sigma m_i^F \mathbf{v}_i^F|=0$, where all the $m_i^F \mathbf{v}_i^F$'s are calculated at $t^F=t^F(s)$ in $(\mathbf{r}^F,t^F)$.

Less formally: draw various time hyperplanes through $(\mathbf{r}_1(s),t(s))$ and find one (the solid hyperplane in Figure 7a) that yields zero total momentum. There is every reason to call the associated frame of reference an *instantaneous rest frame* of the whole object. Then find the radius vector of the center of mass $C^F(s)$ of o at $t^F=t^F(s)$ in $(\mathbf{r}^F,t^F)$: $\mathrm{r}^F_o = \Sigma m_i^F \mathbf{r}_i^F / \Sigma m_i^F$. Now repeat the whole procedure for other values of s. Connect the locations of $C^F(s)$ thus obtained (Figure 7b). Finally, transform the positions $(\mathbf{r}^F_o(s),t^F_o(s))$ of all the $C^F(s)$'s to the original coordinate system $(\mathbf{r},t)$.

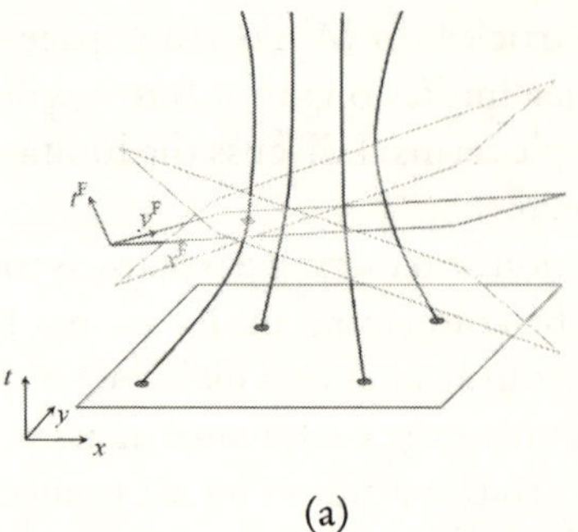

(a)

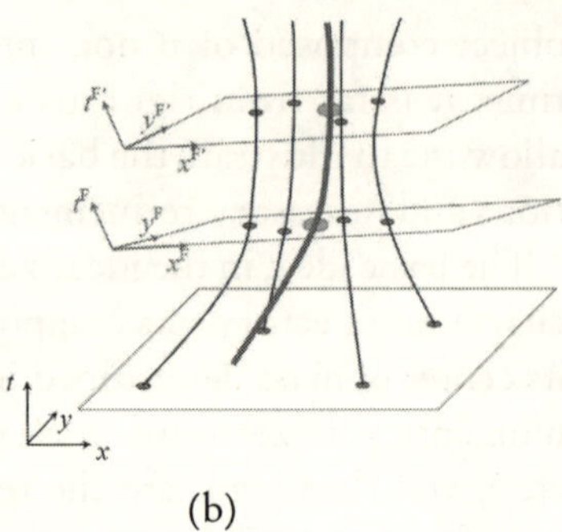

(b)

Figure 7. Toy procedure for drawing the worldline of an arbitrary object composed of *n* non-interacting particles in Minkowski spacetime.

6. Limitations of the Toy Procedure and Rigorous Developments

The toy procedure sketched above is rather convoluted, some steps in any given cycle in it are implicit, and different cycles are not coordinated with each other. Will the procedure generate a unique, continuous and smooth trajectory? The question cannot be answered without undertaking a more rigorous approach.

Some limitations of the toy procedure have to do with neglecting interaction among *o*'s constituent particles. In the absence of interaction, the notion of the common center of mass of o_1, o_2, ... o_n seems to be a somewhat arbitrary quantity without well-defined physical meaning.[8] One way to add some "thickness" to the notion is to associate it with a particular dynamical role perhaps similar to the role of the center of mass in classical mechanics where it is, essentially, the *center of balance*. However, in relativistic mechanics stresses in media are connected with energy densities in unusual ways and themselves contribute to the dynamic mass of the system. Accordingly, there is no way around starting with the stress energy tensor.

An approach (whose details outstrips my expertise) along these lines was developed in a more technical environment by Pryce (1948), and his method was then extended to general relativity by Madore (1969), Dyxon (1970ab), Ehlers and Rudolph (1977), and Schattner (1978; 1979).[9] Pryce begins by considering *six* different methods for defining the center of mass of a system of free particles in special relativity, most of them unsatisfactory, and develops in detail one promising strategy, which he also traces back to Fokker (1929). Pryce then expresses the solution in a form that allows him to extrapolate it to the case of interacting particles. This is done in two steps by starting with a kinematic expression for the four-momentum of a system of n free particles in a given frame:[10]

$$P^{\mu} \equiv \sum_{i=1}^{n} p_i^{\mu} \tag{3}$$

and the following (preliminary) method, whereby the coordinates of the center of mass of the whole system q^{μ} are identified with the mean of the coordinates of the constituent particles q^{μ} weighted with their *relativistic* mass-energies in *that* frame:

$$P^0 q^{\mu} = \sum_i p_i^0 q_i^{\mu} \tag{4}$$

(4) can be usefully viewed as an analog of (2). Pryce then re-expresses in terms of the energy-momentum tensor of a system of free particles

$$T^{\mu\nu}(\mathbf{x}) = \sum_i \int \delta(x^0 - q_i^0)\,\delta(x^1 - q_i^1)\,\delta(x^2 - q_i^2)\,\delta(x^3 - q_i^3)\, p_i^{\mu} dq_i^{\mu} \tag{5}$$

as follows:

$$P^0 q^{\mu} = \iiint x^{\mu} T^{00} dx^1 dx^2 dx^3 \tag{6}$$

which also suggests another tensor quantity $M^{\mu\nu}$ for the role of representing the total angular momentum:

$$M^{\mu\nu} = \iiint (x^{\mu} T^{0\nu} - x^{\nu} T^{0\mu}) dx^1 dx^2 dx^3 \tag{7}$$

This results in a simple expression

$$q^{\mu} = (tP^{\mu} + M^{\mu 0}) / P^0 \tag{8}$$

where $t = x^0$. According to Pryce, (8) "can be applied to a system of particles interacting through a field, thereby removing the original limitation to free particles" (1948, 65).

As it turns out, this simple definition is not independent of the frame of reference. Transforming it to another frame gives rise to extraneous terms. At this point Pryce ties one of the resulting expressions to a frame in which the total momentum vanishes (the zero-momentum frame) and obtains another more complicated expression:

$$q^{\mu} = \frac{tP^{\mu}}{P^{0}} + \frac{M^{\mu\nu}P_{\nu}}{m^{2}} + \frac{M^{\mu 0}P^{\mu}P_{\nu}}{m^{2}P^{0}} \tag{9}$$

"which, in spite of its appearance, is relativistically covariant" (ibid., 65). Here m is the rest mass of the whole system: $m^2 = P^{\mu}P_{\mu}$. I believe (9) is a rigorous counterpart of essentially the same "zero-momentum frame" approach informally outlined in the toy procedure described above – but, of course, without the limitations of the latter.

Based on Pryce's work and some related developments confined to special relativity,[11] several authors – in particular, Dixon (1970ab) and Schattner (1978) – formulated similar strategies in the context of general relativity. Furthermore, Schattner (1979) claims to have established the existence and uniqueness results for his definition of a center-of-mass line for an extended body.

If these developments are correct, how do they square with the worry about non-uniqueness raised by Gibson and Pooley's two-particle case mentioned above? What should disqualify the oblique boldface fragments in Figure 3b from being fragments of a distinct center of mass trajectory of this composite object, alongside the symmetry line of the configuration? Perhaps the neglect of external forces that are needed to make the system perform this sort of motion. Taking such forces into account will require introducing a field that will contribute to the determination of the trajectory of the center of mass, along the lines of Pryce's proposal, and any realistic way of doing so is likely to rule out the oblique fragments.

7. How Much Does It All Matter?

How much does all of that matter in talking about the age of mid-sized ordinary objects in metaphysical discussions about persistence, say? One could agree that the exact determination of the age of spatially extended persisting objects becomes difficult, if not impossible. This can be done only approximately, with a certain "margin or error." The main factor responsible for the vagueness of an object's age is the relative motion of its constituent particles, whereby the ages of different particles get progressively "out of step" with each other, due to relativistic time dilation (the "twins effect" illustrated in Figure 6). How large is this factor?

This question may not have a straightforward answer. Indeed, the answer will depend on the choice of a relevant level of structure. Could tables and chairs (cats and dogs, human beings) be taken to be composed of molecules? Or of atoms? Assuming the former for human beings, the relevant speed can be associated with molecular motion, with a conservative upper bound set at 1 km/sec. This corresponds to $\gamma = 1.000000000006$ and translates into the cumulative time difference (between the "ages" of two molecules in constant relative motion) of mere 0.01 sec over the period of 50 years. One could perhaps rest assured that this sort of indeterminacy is completely innocuous. But of course, molecules are not metaphysical atoms. One needs to go deeper, to physical atoms and subatomic particles. And at that point the situation quickly gets out of control. First of all, things start moving much faster. And one cannot abstract from interaction anymore; indeed, interaction becomes the main contributing factor. And on top of it, the classical non-quantum description ceases to be valid.

But it is good to take one step at a time.[12]

Notes

1 For details, see Balashov (2010, ch. 4).
2 That is, hyperplanes of simultaneity. See Balashov (2010, §5.2) for an argument in favor of such a restriction.
3 Suggested by Cody Gilmore (personal communication).
4 See, in particular, Fokker (1929), Papapetrou (1940), Pryce (1948), Møller (1949), Madore (1969), Dyxon (1970ab), Ehlers and Rudolph (1977), Schattner (1978; 1979), Bailey and Israel (1980), Chryssomalakos et al. (2009), Mermin (2011).
5 My thanks to Oliver Pooley for drawing my attention to these important works.
6 For the latter, see Chryssomalakos et al. (2009). A curious recent development is a short note by N. David Mermin (2011) responding to H. C. Ohanian's claim that Einstein made several mistakes in his famous 1905 derivation of the mass-energy formula. One of these mistakes, according

to Ohanian, includes failure to define the velocity of a composite body, as "there is no obvious 'fiducial point', such as the nonrelativistic center of mass, whose velocity can be used to represent the velocity of the body as a whole" (Mermin 2011, 1). Mermin responds by noting that "if the body is indeed a body – if the internal motions of its parts do not take them more than a bounded distance away from one another – then it is clear how to identify the rest frame to any desired degree of precision. The rest frame is that unique frame in which, no matter how long you wait, part of the body can be found within some bounded region that originally contained the entire body" (ibid.). Mermin concludes, "So there is no problem in defining the velocity of an extended body, even when its parts are in relative motion, and even if their relative velocities are comparable to the speed of light *c*" (ibid.). While this proposal may address a particular issue raised by Ohanian in the context of Einstein's derivation it can hardly serve as a general recipe for defining a unique trajectory representing the motion of an arbitrary composite object in relativistic spacetime. Witness the simple two-body case considered above (Figure 3). My thanks to Geurt Sengers for drawing my attention to Mermin's note.

7 The outline of the toy procedure below follows Balashov (2010, 191–195).

8 Perhaps somewhat similar to the notion of the "center of population" of a country. I thank John Norton for the analogy.

9 I would like to think that despite its obvious limitations the toy model sketched above is in line with these systematic developments. But I will leave it to others to see if the similarity is close enough to use the toy model as a good illustration of the rigorous approach.

10 The outline below of the rigorous procedure closely follows Pryce (1948, 64–65) with some minor change of notation.

11 In particular, Papapetrou (1939), and Møller (1940).

12 This paper is an offshoot of a larger project (Balashov, 2010). My thanks to Oliver Pooley, Nick Huggett, and John Norton for their help, and to Oxford University Press for the permission to use some of the material of section 7.9 of Balashov (2010, 192–195). Versions of the paper were given at the International Workshop on Temporal Existence and Persistence in Spacetime, University-Club Bonn, Germany (February 2011) and the joint Physics/Philosophy Seminar at Idaho State University (Pocatello, Idaho, USA, April 2011). I am grateful to both audiences for very stimulating discussions and to the organizers for their hospitality. Special thanks are due to Cord Friebe, Thomas Müller, and Florian Fischer for their comments on the draft of this paper.

References

Bailey, I./Israel, W., 1980: Relativistic Dynamics of Extended Bodies and Polarized Media: An Eccentric Approach. In: *Annals of Physics* 130, pp. 188–214.

Balashov, Y., 2010: *Persistence and Spacetime*. Oxford: Oxford University Press.

Chryssomalakos, C. et al., 2009: Center of Mass in Special and General Relativity and its Role in an Effective Description of Spacetime. In: *Journal of Physics: Conference Series* 174, pp. 1–4.

Dyxon, W. G., 1970ab: Dynamics of Extended Bodies in General Relativity. In *Proceedings of the Royal Society of London* 314A, pp. 499–527; and 319A, pp. 509–547.

Ehlers, J./Rudolph, E., 1977: Dynamics of Extended Bodies in General Relativity: Center-of-Mass Description and Quasirigidity. In *General Relativity and Gravitation* 8, pp. 197–217.

Fokker, A. D., 1929: *Relativitätstheorie*. Groningen: P. Noordhoff.

Gibson, I./Pooley, O., 2006: Relativistic Persistence. In: Hawthorne, J. (ed.), *Philosophical Perspectives*, Vol. 20, *Metaphysics*. Oxford: Blackwell, pp. 157–198.

Gilmore, C., 2008: Persistence and Location in Relativistic Spacetime. In: *Philosophy Compass* 3 (6), pp. 1224–54.

Madore, J., 1969: The Equations of Motion of an Extended Body in General Relativity. In: *Annales de l'institut Henri Poincaré* (A) Physique théorique 11A, pp. 221–237.

Mermin, N. D., 2011: Understanding Einstein's 1905 derivation of $E=Mc^2$. In: *Studies in History and Philosophy of Modern Physics* 42, pp. 1–2.

Møller, C., 1949: In: *Commun. Dublin Inst. Adv. Stud.* A, No. 5.

Papapetrou, A., 1939: Drehimpuls- und Schwerpunktsatz in der relativistischen Mechanik. In: *Praktika of the Academy of Athenes* 14, p. 540.

Pryce, M. H. L., 1948: The Mass-Centre in the Restricted Theory of Relativity and Its Connexion with the Quantum Theory of Elementary Particles. In: *Proceedings of the Royal Society of London* 195A, pp. 62–81.

Schattner, R., 1978: The Center of Mass in General Relativity. In: *General Relativity and Gravitation* 10, pp. 377–393.

Schattner, R., 1979: The Uniqueness of the Center of Mass in General Relativity. In: *General Relativity and Gravitation* 10, pp. 395–399.

Mauro Dorato

Presentism/Eternalism and Endurantism/Perdurantism: why the Unsubstantiality of the first debate implies that of the second[1]

Abstract

The main claim that I want to defend in this paper is that there are logical equivalences between eternalism and perdurantism on the one hand and presentism and endurantism on the other. By "logical equivalence" I mean that one position is entailed and entails the other. As a consequence of these equivalences, it becomes important to inquire into the question whether the dispute between endurantists and perdurantists is authentic, given that Savitt (2006) Dolev (2006) and Dorato (2006) have cast doubts on the fact that the debate between presentism and eternalism is about "what there is". In this respect, I will conclude that also the debate about persistence in time has no ontological consequences, in the sense that there is no real ontological disagreement between the two allegedly opposite positions: as in the case of the presentism/eternalism debate, one can be both a perdurantist and an endurantist, depending on which linguistic framework is preferred.

Zusammenfassung

Die Hauptthese dieses Aufsatzes ist, dass logische Äquivalenzen zwischen Eternalismus und Perdurantismus, auf der einen Seite, und Präsentismus und Endurantismus, auf der anderen Seite, bestehen. „Logisch äquivalent" sind sie, weil die jeweils erste Position die zweite impliziert und von ihr impliziert ist. Als Konsequenz dieser Äquivalenzen stellt sich die Frage, ob es sich bei dem Streit zwischen Endurantisten und Perdurantisten um einen gehaltvollen handelt, da ja jüngst Savitt (2006), Dolev (2006) und Dorato (2006) in Zweifel gezogen haben, dass die Debatte um Präsentismus und Eternalismus eine ist über ‚was es gibt'. Vor diesem Hintergrund folgere ich, dass auch die Debatte um zeitliche Persistenz keine ontologischen Konsequenzen hat, in dem Sinne, dass zwischen den vermeintlich gegensätzlichen Positionen kein wirklicher ontologischer Unterschied besteht: Wie im Falle der Präsentismus/Eternalismus-Debatte kann man sowohl Perdurantist als auch Endurantist sein, je nachdem, welches Sprachsystem man bevorzugt.

The main claim that I want to defend in this paper is that there are logical equivalences between eternalism and perdurantism on the one hand and presentism and endurantism on the other. By "logical equivalence" I mean that one position is entailed and entails the other. As a consequence of these equivalences, it becomes important to inquire into the question whether the dispute between endurantists and perdurantists is authentic, given that Savitt (2006) Dolev (2006) and Dorato (2006) have cast doubts on the fact that the debate between presentism and eternalism is about "what there is". In this respect, I will conclude that also the debate about persistence in time has no ontological consequences, in the sense that there is no real ontological disagreement between the two allegedly opposite positions: as in the case of the presentism/eternalism debate, one can be *both* a perdurantist and an endurantist, depending on which linguistic framework is preferred. More in detail, I will defend the following equivalence: in the case of the presentism/eternalism debate, present-tense expressions have the aim of expressing the temporal position of the speaker *vis à vis* the events one is referring to; but in other circumstances, by using a tenseless copula, one is taking a sort of an non-perspectival, view-from-nowhere outlook *vis à vis* past, present and future events, by declaring them to be all *tenselessly* coexistent. Both uses of the copula (tensed and tenseless) are consistent and important, so that there is no reason to transform the choice of a language into a philosophical dispute about what there is. Analogous conclusion will be show to hold for the endurantist/perdurantism dispute.

In particular, in section 1 of the paper I will defend the above mentioned equivalence, while in section 2 I will show in what sense, in virtue of the equivalence, one could argue that if presentism/eternalism is a pseudo-debate *on the ontological level*, because both a presentist and an eternalist language are appropriate in different circumstances, then so is the endurantist/perdurantist issue. In section 3, finally, I will argue that the issue of persistence in time, exactly as that between presentism and eternalism, makes a very superficial use of physics: philosophers try to use the prestige of the latter in order to give some substance to purely a priori debates, a philosophical approach which runs the risk of creating a new scholastics. Such an irrelevance is, I take it, an independent argument against the importance of the metaphysical debate about persistence in time, not because metaphysics should not pursue investigations in issues that science cannot settle, but because the use of physics in the debate in question is external and superimposed.

1. A chain of logical equivalences

Just to fix terminology, in the remainder of this paper I will assume that eternalism is committed to the *tenseless coexistence* of all *events*, while presentism is committed to the thesis that existence is confined just to the *present* events, while future and past events do not exist. In order to show the logical equivalences mentioned above, I will take perdurantism as the doctrine that *all entities* persist in time by having temporal parts, while endurantism will be regarded as the doctrine that *all entities* have no temporal parts, so that they all persist in time by being "wholly present" when they exist.

Two important remarks are appropriate before entering *in medias res*. 1) I presented endurantism as the negation of perdurantism: whether a third alternative to these two doctrines is available is an interesting question that here will not be discussed. 2) The presentist/eternalist debate is often formulated as involving only *events*, while the issue of persistence in time is typically taken to concern only *things*. In the definition above I considered "entity" as a general term that applies to *both* things and events. This terminological choice, however, needs some justification. On the one hand, admittedly, if events and things were two irreducible ontic categories, we would have *prima facie* evidence against the possibility of using the above mentioned equivalence to shed light on the meaningfulness of the endurantist/perdurantism debate. On the other hand, however, *if*, at least at the beginning, we leave the issue of the ontic dualism about entities and things open, and *if* the equivalence I am after is correct, as I think it is, two possible consequence could result, neither of which need to be tackled here:

(i) either also talk of things and talk of events ends up being inter-translatable, so that events and things ought not to be regarded as individuating two different ontological categories,

(ii) or there are two different ways in which individual entities persist in time, *things* by enduring and *events* by perduring, so that perdurantism and endurantism are both true, in a sense not altogether different from that in which, in my opinion, presentism and eternalism are both true in different circumstances.

In the former option (i), the pluralistic claim that *some* entities (things) persist by enduring and others (events) persist by perduring would have to be abandoned, and my final claim will be independently motivated by the ontological equivalence of those entities that are typically regarded as perduring (events) and those that are typically regarded as enduring (things). In the latter alternative (ii), *pluralism* would turn out be the right way of interpreting the debate,[2] but in this case the interest of the debate, which in the formulation above I took to be about *all* persisting entities, would be deflated in the direction that here is argued for and defended.

1.1 How to prove that endurantism entails presentism[3]

Let me label endurantism as defined above with "END" and presentism with "PRES"; ETER stands for eternalism and PER for perdurantism. In this section I will show that END → PRES. Assume endurantism: it follows that entities have no temporal parts (this feature, I have assumed, is essential to endurantism). If entities have no temporal parts, then:

1) they are 3-dimensional;
2) they possess only *spatial* parts;
3) they *exist* wholly at each moment in which they exist.

Let us focus on condition 3), and on the current debate whether in general "exist" is or is not ambiguous between tensed and tenseless existence. In temporal contexts one can always raise the question whether "exist" is meant in the tensed or in the tenseless sense of existence, so that existence in 3) is indeed ambiguous. If entities exist wholly at each moment of their existence, then:

(a) Entities can either exist only in the present (presentism), or

(b) There are (tenselessly coexisting) moments in the past and in the future, at each of which entities wholly exist (eternalism); if both of these linguistic[4] options were compatible with endurantism – that is, if (END & PRES) and (END & ETER) were both true – my claim that presentism is derivable from endurantism would be false.

However, I will now show that my claim is not false. If (a) is the case, the sought-after implication (endurantism → presentism, or END → PRES) is proven. If (b) is the case, the tenseless coexistence of moments of past and future times at each of which the *same* entity wholly exist seems to drive us toward the existence of "durationless" *temporal parts* of the entity, against our assumption of END.

To understand why this conclusion follows, assume *per absurdum* that endurantism be compatible with eternalism (END & ETER) and consider two "things" at a certain time, for instance, "me at the present moment", or "the Mount Everest at the present moment". By endurantist hypothesis, both I and the Mount Everest now have no temporal parts and now exist wholly (whatever that means, see *infra*). "Me-at-past-time-t" and "me-at-future-time-t", however, also don't have temporal parts, but, on the assumption that eternalism be consistent with endurantism, *they would tenselessly coexist with me-now*. Given such a tenseless coexistence, however, "I" might end up being constituted by my complete history or by the totality of my different temporal parts (past, present and future "stages"). Each of these stages would have no temporal parts because they can be regarded as having no temporal duration. Since by assuming endurantism we assumed lack of temporal parts, but eternalism entails the existence of tenselessly coexisting temporal parts, if I (a *prima facie* "thing") am constituted by, or identical with, my history (*prima facie* "events"), we are forced to accept that also on hypothesis (b) endurantism → presentism (END → PRES).

One could object that an indexing of entities to (proper) time or (coordinate) time, i.e., descriptions of the sort "me at the present moment", ought to be banned by endurantists and are therefore question-begging. One cannot "relativize" to time entities which, by hypothesis, have no temporal parts: that is, it could be objected that for the endurantist there are no such things as "me-now" or "my future-self", but only me, existing wholly by being multilocated at different regions of spacetime. However, it is not clear why "me (or my body) at t", or "Mount Everest at t" should be unconceivable or banned in an endurantistic language, since also endurantists *must* be able to consider the existence of enduring entities at certain instants of time. Endurantists could of course admit the necessity of using our language in this way, but claim at the same time that such a use is referentially empty, thereby assigning a purely *instrumental* value to the time-indexing of Mount Everest or of me. But the claim "Mount Everest in 1911 was devoid of human traces, while Mount Everest in 2011 is full of them" is certainly true, and the truth makers of this assertion *can* be regarded either (a) as different, tenselessly coexisting temporal parts or slices of the selfsame persisting entity or (b) as two different properties instantiated by the same thing/substance at different times. In the former hypothesis (a), the endurantist that embraces eternalism must embrace the tenseless coexistence of temporal parts of Mount Everest, and therefore abandon her view that things have no temporal parts. So END entails PRES, as wanted.

In the second hypothesis (b), the eternalist endurantist must concede that different properties exemplified by the same substance at two different times-places are different *events* (this is Kim's 1976 view of events). Such events, by occurring *to* the very same substance and by happening at different times, must be regarded as tenselessly coexistent (in virtue of eternalism). But if these events coexist tenselessly, nothing prevents one from arguing that they *can* be regarded as different temporal parts of the same mountain, so that there is nothing over and above the mountain than its full history, that is, the set of all events that occur to it. The typical monistic argument against the independent existence of substances (or things) runs in fact as follows: what is, after all, this *empirically undetectable* substance to which all attributes or properties would inhere if not a projection of the subject-predicate structure of our language onto reality that need *not* be mirrored by the structure of entities?[5] While of course the discussion on this issue could and should continue, I will stop it here, since my purpose is not to solve the debate on the independent existent of things *vis à vis* that of events, but rather only to show that alternative characterizations of things/substances in terms of events are *always* possible. And this is *enough* to conclude that since eternalism implies the existence of temporal parts and we started by assuming endurantism, we are able to conclude that endurantism → presentism also on reading (b) of 3) above, which, it will be recalled, is the feature of enduring entities such that "they exists wholly at each times in which they exist".

Summarizing the whole argument developed in this section, if endurantism (END) were first assumed and then regarded as consistent with eternalism (ETER), we would have a contradiction, because eternalism implies the existence of temporal parts for all entities (things or events). It follows that eternalism cannot be compatible with END. In symbols: $\neg(\text{END} \ \& \ \text{ETER}) \rightarrow (\text{END} \rightarrow \neg\text{ETER}) \rightarrow (\text{END} \rightarrow \text{PRES})$

1.2 Why also presentism entails endurantism (PRES → END)

Suppose that there is a way to formulate presentism in a non-trivial fashion, so that presentism does not oscillate between a tensed triviality ("all that exists now exists now") and a tenseless contradiction ("whatever existed in the past or exists now or will exist in the future does not tenselessly exist, that is, it has not existed nor does it exist now nor will it exist").[6] *Prima facie*, if whatever exists exists now (as presentism has it), so that all that exists coexist in the same spatial hypersurface, then there *are* – in some very general sense of "there are", if, controversially, there is such a general, unique existential quantification as Sider (2001) has it – no past or future parts of entities. To the extent that it makes sense to claim, along with presentists, that there are no past or future parts of entities, then there are also no temporal parts of them (endurantism). If presentism has a genuine linguistic formulation, then also the conclusion presentism → endurantism follows (PRES → ETER).

My point here is that we cannot conclude from the fact that presentism is neither a triviality nor a contradiction that there is a genuine ontological divide between presentism and eternalism, and it is this latter thesis that I deny, since the two different ways of looking at events in time (perspectivally as in presentism and non-perspectivally as in eternalism) do not exclude each other at all, and are both useful and important in different contexts.[7]

An objection against the claim that presentism entails endurantism springs to mind naturally, and involves transtemporal identity: one could ask whether (i) the now-existing entity *e* will exist also in the future by preserving its identity, or (ii) e-now is a temporal part of a temporally extended entity *E*, which will have another part *e′* in the future, where $e \neq e'$. In the former case (i), the now-existing entity *endures* because it preserves its identity at different times (and my thesis is proved), in the latter case (ii), however, there *will* exist a different part of *E* at a future time (perdurantism), so that presentism and perdurantism, against my claim, seem to be wholly compatible.

In order to meet this objection, let us suppose *per absurdum* that presentism and perdurantism be compatible.[8] Perdurantism requires the existence of a relation of "parthood" (*x* and *y* are parts of *E*) among the temporal parts of any temporally extended, persisting entity, so that the presentist's claim that only the present part exists is more than seriously threatened. The fact is that *the parts of a temporally extended entity E can be related* (i.e., the parts or stages can instantiate a relation of parthood) – as required by perdurantism – *only if their relata all coexist tenselessly*, as eternalists have it. Relations can exist only if their relata do. Since perdurantism entails eternalism but we started by assuming presentism, we have derived a contradiction; so we'd better conclude that presentism entails endurantism.[9]

On the assumption that presentism and endurantism are equivalent or imply each other, the same holds for eternalism and perdurantism, at least if ¬ eternalism = presentism (no growing block view of reality, where only the future is unreal) and ¬ endurantism = perdurantism. In order to further convince ourselves of the equivalence of these views, however, it is instructive to look into the converse implications, involving endurantism and eternalism.

1.3 Why eternalism entails perdurantism (ETER → PERD)

Assume eternalism. If all entities coexist in a tenseless sense (as eternalism preaches), any entity having more than an instantaneous existence has either (i) different temporal parts at different times and therefore perdures, or (ii) persists by enduring, that is, by existing wholly at each instants in which it exists. Since (i) proves my case, let us consider (ii), i.e., the possibility that the selfsame entity *E* persists at two different times t_1 and t_2 by "existing wholly" at each of these times (endurantism), without having temporal parts.

Now the thorny question arises: what does "existing wholly" mean in this case, other than the fact that *E* has no temporal parts? There is an important sense in which *E* does *not* exist wholly at t_1, since the very same enduring *E* also exists at t_2. This follows because it is always possible to treat *E* at t_1 and *E* at t_2 as two different stages or temporal parts of the very same *E*. In full analogy, in the theory of universals there is a sense in which if there are two different instantiations of the very same property *P*, *P* does not exist fully in any of these instances, because the very same P can be regarded as the disjoint sum of *all* its instantiations in spacetime. It exists fully in all of its instances in the sense that it is identical with itself (the same P) in all of its instances.

Going back to our business, it is because we need a relation of genidentity for different stages of the same temporally extended event that eternalism entails the existence of temporal parts and therefore perdurantism (ETER → PERD). If it were not possible to identify at different times the same entity, the eternalist would have no way to claim that two stages or slices are indeed stages or slices of the *same* entity, and this is essential in any metaphysical doctrine of persistence through time.

But even if this re-identification were not possible, and if worries about bare particulars as carriers of identity could be dispensed, so that an entity could be regarded as something over and above the set of events that *occur to it* at a given time, one could press the following, additional point. "existing wholly at each moment of its existence" might mean that "entity *E* is wholly present at each of these moments" in the temporal sense, which, in turns, is possible if and only if *E* has no future or past parts at each moment in which it exists. This formulation of endurantism, however, pushes energically toward presentism: "*E* is wholly present at *t*" ends up meaning that "for all instants *t*, *E* exists just when *t* = now", which is a non-standard way of formulating presentism, but presentism nonetheless. However, (i) we assumed eternalism; (ii) the assumption of compatibility between eternalism and endurantism leads to presentism; in order to avoid a contradiction, we must conclude that eternalism entails perdurantism (ETER → PERD).

The argument in favor of the implication of eternalism by perdurantism is much easier to establish and has already been given: the relation of parthood among parts of temporally extended entities required by perdurantism ("x and y are temporal part of *E*") implies the tenseless coexistence of the temporal parts, and therefore eternalism; the implication from perdurantism to eternalism is therefore secured (PERD → ETER).

2. The consequences of the logical equivalence

If endurantism is logically equivalent to presentism, and perdurantism to eternalism, and if the presentism/eternalism is not a genuine ontological debate (as Savitt, Dolev, and Dorato have it, see above), it could be maintained that the endurantism-perdurantism debate comes out as non-genuine too: not because the latter two positions are intertranslatable (Miller, 2005), but because endurantism and perdurantism are, respectively, logically equivalent to two ontologically compatible positions.

How plausible is this conclusion? It is important to understand the way in which presentism and eternalism can coexist, despite the fact that they *seem* to advocate ontologically distinct positions. Suppose that, *qua* presentist, I want to claim that only what is presently existing exists. Independently of the difficulty of determining what counts as present within a given spacetime (a single pointlike event, a hypersurface of simultaneity, the null cone, the spacelike-related region to a point, etc.),[10] there is no reason why a presentist should *not* accept that *some* events *will exist* (if now is not the last moment of time, or Big Crunch) and other events *have existed* (if now is not the first moment of time, or Big Bang).[11] However, this is exactly what a reasonable eternalist should advocate. At least if we construe eternalism as the doctrine that any two entities coexist tenselessly if and only if they are part of the same spacetime, or if and only if one of the two entities will exist relative to the other, or both exist simultaneously, or one has existed relative to the other, where the past or the future tense is determined with respect to some instant of proper (STR)[12] or cosmic time (GTR). In other words, there is no reason why an eternalist should not accept that inside a four-dimensional space-time, and relative to a given event, some events will exist and other have existed, as the presentist wants, *modulo* reference to local or global proper time, depending on the spacetime we want to consider. So where is the ontological difference between the two positions? While for the defense of this version of eternalism I refer the reader to the previously mentioned papers, here it will suffice to say that a future or a past event, relatively to a given now, do not now exist also for an eternalist, given that they will exist and have existed. Independently of questions related to what form the truth conditions of tensed sentences should take, once the tensed and tenseless form of existence or of the copula are carefully separated, very little discussion remains, since the choice of one rather than of the other form of the copula boils down to a pragmatic question. Sometimes (very often and I daresay in most cases) we need to distinguish what exists now from what exists elsewhen (and then we use the tensed copula). Some other times, however, especially when we write physical theories or when we need to distinguish the concrete existence in spacetime from fictional existence, we use the tenseless copula, by referring to whole set of concrete events located somewhere in spacetime.

In a word, the argument against the ontological significance of the debate on how entities persist in time is as follows. Given the logical equivalence defended above, it would seem that *if* the perdurantists/endurantists debate has to have ontic significance, it must have ontic significance also the presentist/eternalist debate.[13] But since on the basis of previous work we are here assuming that the latter debate need not amount to a disagreement about ontology, the former debate also amounts to two different ways of describing persistence in time, with no ontological implications.[14]

If this is correct, we need to answer the following question: why does it look as if there is genuine ontological dispute between perdurantists and endurantists? The origin of the dispute lies, *at least in part*, in the fact that some entities change much more slowly than others. The slowly changing Mount Everest looks like an entity whose existence is "wholly present" at each moment in which it exists, so that its identity seems to remain unchanged across time: it looks as if there are no past or future parts of mountains! A concert, on the other hand, is a process having quick changes, so that it looks as if it has temporal parts that succeed one another. However, depending on our descriptive aims, Mount Everest can be regarded as a set of temporal parts (say, a geologist can be interested in the early stage of the formation of the mountain), and at the same time a whole concert can be regarded as having a trans-temporal identity in virtue of relations of genidentity or of the region it occupies in spacetime, while its temporal slices, when they exist, exist wholly simply because they are durationless.

Of course, a friend of the distinction perdurantism/endurantism would object that one can imagine a balloon (a purported substance which persists by enduring) *quickly* changing by deflating or inflating: these are *events* which occur to the enduring balloon, which however persist in time in a way that differs from the way in which its inflation or deflation persist. While one can of course choose this way of speaking, it is not clear what its ontological consequences are. In fact, what remains of the balloon after we consider all the events that take place "in" (?) it at a given moment of time? What sort of non-empirical heacceity remains after we remove all the time-indexed properties (events) from an object? Such an heacceity is certainly not a qualitative property on a par with the others, and it is doubtful whether it exists. On the other hand, if we consider a thunderstorm, such a paradigmatically perduring entity also has an identity to which we are typically less interested. However, if need arises, we can trace such an identity either to the event's spatiotemporal location, or to its properties, or to its causes and effects, or to whatever it is that we consider relevant in a given circumstance. In any case, in these cases the problem involves the identity of an entity more than the way in which it persists in time, even though the two questions are related.

3. Against a superficial use of physics: the argument from irrelevance

Even if all I wrote so far were wrong, it is important to remind ourselves that physics does not aim at establishing whether entities persist in time by perduring or enduring. This is not a problem that physicists are currently after. So no deep interactions between physics and metaphysics on the basis of the metaphysical dispute we are discussing seem forthcoming. I don't know of a possible development of physics that might render the current discussion about persistence in time relevant for a deeper understanding of the implication of the physics of time. Four-dimensionalism can be used to explain relativistic effects structurally, and reference to the present stage of expansion via cosmic time (a three-dimensional outlook) is also important for pragmatic reasons, as when we claim that the universe is now 14.6 billion years old. These pragmatic differences, however, do not seem to amount to an ontological divide between three-dimensionalism and four-dimensionalism. Even though in certain circumstances one way of speaking is preferred to another, attributing this pragmatic difference an ontological significance does not make any difference in our understanding current physical theories.

It could be objected that the aim of the metaphysics of time is not to contribute to a deeper understanding of time in physics. Rather, the idea is that one develops a metaphysical theory of persistence and then judges its plausibility in terms of logical and empirical consistency. "Empirical consistency" means, typically, that physics is used to adjudicate a metaphysical debate by eliminating or weakening one of the two contenders *via* compatibility arguments. However, certain philosophical discussions based on compatibility arguments tend to forget that physics underdetermines many metaphysical debates. Underdetermination seems to strike metaphysical disputes about three or four dimensionalism, or presentism and eternalism. It is always possible to introduce –

for purely metaphysical reasons, and on the hypothesis that current physics is incomplete – a privileged but empirically undetectable reference frame that does not contradict the special theory of relativity, *qua scientific* theory. Such an empirically inaccessible inertial frame would do the job that presentists or three-dimensionalists are after. The introduction of a privileged inertial frame for metaphysical reasons cannot be prohibited on physical reasons alone, even if it amounts to a very artificial tampering with a physical theory for purely metaphysical reasons that I would not recommend. What matters here, however, is that such a tampering *per se* does nothing to contribute to a deeper understanding of the current problems of time in physics (the origin of the arrow of time, the problem of establishing whether time exists at a fundamental level, the nature of cosmic time in its relation with becoming, whether time had a beginning, etc.).

In order to close in a more constructive fashion, I want to briefly propose a way to build a more fruitful relationship between physics and metaphysics by advancing the following interpretive project. In my view, interpreting physical theories could be regarded as a two stage project[15]:

1) Coming up with a precise and exact ontology (in the sense of Bell) to associate with the language and formulas of physical theories;

2) Relating such ontology to the world of our experience.

These are the two inseparable tasks of metaphysicians and philosophers of physics, rendered indispensible by the frequent clash between the scientific (physical) image and the manifest image of the world (Sellars, 1963). The question of the possibly conflicting relationship of the ontology of physics with that of our experience can arise only if the ontology of physics is taken at face value. It is only if the table is really made of atoms that the question of the relationship of the empty physical table with the hard and colored table of our experience can be posed at all (Eddington, 1927). Both instrumentalism about physics and eliminationism about our conscious experience, however, are too easy way outs, and therefore no solutions to the problem of interpreting physical theories as articulated in 1) and 2). A quickly discussed example will illustrate the significance of the interpretive projects above.

As to 1): Finding out whether the universe becomes in time, for instance, is not an idle metaphysical game, since it is linked to interpretations of the nature of time in Special Relativity, General Relativity and Quantum Gravity. For instance: what is the nature of cosmic time in cosmology? Does it allow some form of becoming of the universe that is objective? This question needs of course a precise explication of the intuitive notion of becoming.

The second point 2 is linked to a deeper understanding of the relationship between becoming and the various arrows of time in physics: if there is becoming, how is it linked to the other arrows of time? This problem it is linked to the need of relating the world of our experience, where time passes, to the world of physics in an explanatory fashion. For instance, suppose that the present is local and not global as the special theory of relativity seems to force us to acknowledge. Is it possible to explain the illusion of a cosmic present via our neurophysiological perception of time?

As a sketch of an explanation, consider that we cannot perceive the present but only the past of events: we believe in the global nature of the present moment because of (1) the speed of light *c* (300.000 km/s) and (2) the threshold time needed for perceiving the temporal succession of light signals (approximately 30ms). It follows that in a sphere of a radius of 9000 km (*c* times 30ms) we cannot perceive temporal succession, but only simultaneous events! If we want to create less superficial contacts between physics and metaphysics, we need to realize that the latter is an elaboration of the manifest image of the world, in which cognitive and neurophysiological sciences, beside conceptual apriori analysis, have an important role.

In a word, lest our philosophy becomes less and less in touch with real science, we need to stop worrying about problems that have no relevance for physics and rather try to form a synoptic view of the world in which the true task is connecting 1) with 2). This is only *a* way to pursue metaphysics of science, of course: let thousands of flowers bloom.

Notes

1 My thanks to Florian Fischer, Cord Friebe, Thomas Müller and Thorben Petersen for their valuable comments and criticism concerning a previous version of this paper. All remaining errors are my responsibility.

2 Such a pluralism is defended in Mellor (1981).

3 For papers connecting the persistence debate with presentism and eternalism, see Merricks (1995 and 1999), and Rea (1998).

4 Here "linguistic" is important, since it serves to signal that the distinction between presentism and eternalism concerns two different ways of reading existence, both admissible and useful, and not ontology, since in different linguistic contexts we talk like a presentist and in others like an eternalist. *I am not assuming that presentist talk is translatable into eternalist talk.*

5 It could be maintained that the relation between a substance and its time-indexed properties (events) is no more mysterious than the relation between a perduring, temporally extended event and its non time-indexed properties. An *exciting* party (an entity with temporal parts) need not have this non-time indexed property ("being exciting") at all times in which it exists, but it certainly must instantiate it at various stages of the party. There is nothing mysterious in this. On the contrary, a substance without events occurring to it at all times in which it exists, i.e., a substance without time-indexed properties, would be a mere nothing, in the same sense in which an abstract temporal part without properties would be nothing at all.

6 The contradiction is generated by reading the copula "is" in the statement of presentism – "the future event *E* is unreal"- as a tenseless "is", amounting to "was, is now, or will be the case". So my (future) death *is* unreal would mean that "it did not take place, it is not taking place now, nor will it take place", which is clearly false, because it will take place, something that also the presentist will concede, of course. On the other hand, "the future event *E* is now (tensed copula) not real" is clearly trivially true, because what will occur (the future event *E*) is not occurring now! (I assume here that the truth-condition of utterance U= "event E is now not real" is given by the tenseless statement "E does not occur simultaneous with U", even though this truth condition and U mean different things).

7 See Dolev (2006), Dorato (2006), and Savitt (2006), quoted above, that in different ways argue in favor of the dissolution of the presentist/eternalist debate at an ontic level. See also Dorato (2006a) for a corresponding deflationary thesis on absolute becoming and its *apriori* character, presupposed by all spacetime theories relying on an ontology of events.

8 Brogaard (2000) is a defense of a fourdimensionalist type of presentism, that is, of the idea that a presentist can believe in temporal parts and therefore in perdurantism. See also Miller (2009).

9 Another possible view on the matter is that presentists cannot have any theory of persistence, since reality is constituted by instantaneous slices (the nows) which succeed one another without either enduring or perduring. However, if I am a presentist, I would want to persist in time, in such a way that either my present stage be causally connected with my future stages (perdurantism), or in such a way that I endure in time by keeping my identity across my life. So presentism without some form of persistence in time is only compatible with a radical form of occasionalistic metaphysics, in which the world is created anew at each instant of time, and identity is merely illusory.

10 See Savitt (2000).

11 A presentist might object that referring to the first or last moment of time makes reference to B time, as for a presentist the beginning (end) of time is the beginning (end) of the present. (I owe this objection to Cord Friebe). However, a presentist must be able to describe a cosmology in which the Universe has a finite duration in time and began 14,6 billions years ago. That is, it must be able to refer to the existence of past entities in some sense. Difficulties to have truth-conditions for non-present tense sentences must, and can be overcome.

12 Temporal succession is not annihilated even in Minkowski spacetime: it becomes local.

13 For the purpose of the paper, one side of the biconditional suffice for the argument, namely for the thesis that perdurantism entails eternalism and endurantism entails presentism.

14 Of course the implication could be used in the converse form: if the presentist/eternalist debate had a genuine ontological character, also the perdurantist/endurantist debate would!

15 For more details, see Dorato (2010).

References

Broogard, Berit, 2000: Presentist Four-Dimensionalism. In: *The Monist* 83 (3), pp. 341–356.

Dolev, Yuval, 2006: How to Square a Non-Localized Present with Special Relativity. In: Dieks, Dennis (ed.): *The Ontology of Spacetime*. Amsterdam: Elsevier, pp. 177–190.

Dorato, Mauro, 2006: The irrelevance of the presentism/eternalism debate for the ontology of Minkowski spacetime. In: Dieks, Dennis (ed.): *The Ontology of Spacetime*. Amsterdam: Elsevier, pp. 93–109.

Dorato, Mauro, 2006a: Absolute becoming, relational becoming and the arrow of time: Some non conventional remarks on the relationship between physics and metaphysics. In: *Studies in History and Philosophy of Modern Physics* 37 (3), pp. 559–576.

Dorato, Mauro, 2010: Physics and Metaphysics: Interaction or Autonomy?, In: Calosi, Claudio (ed): *Physics and Metaphysics, Humana-Mente* 13, Pisa: ETS, pp. 1–11.

Eddington, Arthur, 1927: *The Nature of the Physical World* [Gifford Lectures, University of Edinburgh, January-March 1927]. Reprinted, 1958: Ann Arbor: University of Michigan Press.

Kim, Jaegwon, 1976: Events as Property Exemplifications. In Brand, M./Walton, D. (eds.), *Action Theory*. Dordrecht: Reidel, pp. 159–77.

Mellor, David, 1981: *Real Time*. Cambridge: Cambridge University Press.

Merricks, Trenton, 1995: On the incompatibility of Enduring and Perduring Entities. In: *Mind* 104, pp. 523-531

Merricks, Trenton, 1999: Persistence, Parts and Presentism. In: *Noûs* 33, pp. 421–38.

Miller, Kristie, 2005: The Metaphysical Equivalence of Three and Four Dimensionalism. In: *Erkenntnis* 62 (1), pp. 91–117.

Miller, Kristie, 2009: Ought a fourdimensionalist to believe in temporal parts?, In: *Canadian Journal of Philosophy* 39 (4), pp. 619–646.

Rea, Michael, 1998: Temporal Parts Unmotivated. In: *Philosophical Review* 107, pp. 225–60.

Savitt, Steven, 2000: There's No Time Like the Present (in Minkowski Spacetime). In: *Philosophy of Science* 67 (Proceedings), pp. S563–S574.

Savitt, Steven, 2006: Presentism and Eternalism in Perspective. In: Dieks, Dennis (ed.): *The Ontology of Spacetime*. Amsterdam: Elsevier, pp. 111–127.

Sellars, Wilfrid, 1963: *Science, Perception and Reality*. London: Routledge & Kegan Paul.

Sider, Ted, 2001: *Fourdimensionalism. An Ontology of Persistence and Time*. Oxford: Oxford University Press.

Florian Fischer

On the Asymmetry of Endurantistic and Perdurantistic Coexistence in Special Relativity

Abstract

The paper reviews Balashov's Asymmetry Thesis concerning co-existing (point-sized) enduring objects, on the one hand, and perduring ones, on the other. In this regard, it becomes crucial to investigate whether, at a given spacetime point p, it is located only the respective temporal part of a perduring whole, or that whole as well. Two alternatives ought to be distinguished and, then, I will argue as follows:
If the perduring whole is located where its parts are, the original asymmetry-thesis has to be rejected. If, however, the perduring whole is not located where its parts are, the spatiotemporal locations of the parts can no longer be used to ground the co-existence relation. But, with the modified co-existence relation the asymmetry between perdurantism and endurantism turns out to be even much stronger than it has been assumed.

Zusammenfassung

Untersucht wird Balashovs Asymmetrie-These zwischen koexistierenden (punktartigen) endurierenden Objekten auf der einen Seite und perdurierenden auf der anderen. Dabei ist es entscheidend abzuwägen, ob an einem bestimmten Raumzeitpunkt p nur der zeitliche Teil eines perdurierenden Objektes lokalisiert ist oder auch das Objekt selbst. Es werden zwei Fälle unterschieden und gezeigt:
Wenn das perdurierende Ganze dort lokalisiert ist, wo seine Teile sind, muss die ursprüngliche Asymmetrie-These zurückgewiesen werden. Ist das perdurierende Ganze hingegen nicht dort, wo seine Teile sind, dann kann die raumzeitliche Position der Teile nicht als Basis für die Koexistenz-Relation fungieren. Mit dem modifizierten Koexistenz-Begriff erweist sich die Asymmetrie zwischen Perdurantismus und Endurantismus aber als weitaus stärker als bislang angenommen.

1. Introduction

The nature of persistence is a controversial business, although it is a pretty common phenomenon that objects persist through time. There has been a long debate concerning the different accounts of persistence in analytic philosophy.[1] Meanwhile some philosophers of spacetime physics hold that considering the Special Theory of Relativity (SR) could add some ground on which to decide for or against one theory. Yuri Balashov, for example has put forward *a posteriori* arguments against eternalistic endurantism. In general, there must be some kind of asymmetry between the theories at stake, to ground any argument. In one approach, considering the coexistence of spatially unextended persisting objects in Minkowski spacetime, this asymmetry was associated with so-called tensed determinations. The endurantists, it is argued, are committed to claims like 'object a is still in existence for object b', where 'still' is one of the mentioned tensed determinations, which is allegedly incompatible with SR.

After rephrasing the original argument from Balashov and the reactions to it[2], I will demonstrate that the stated asymmetry cannot be held up. The purported argument crucially relies on a thesis about the different localisations of enduring and perduring objects. Instead of arguing for or against this thesis in general, I will consider its truth and falsehood in a case-by-case analysis.

The aim of this paper is not to reject the argument from SR against endurantism, but to clarify the accounts of persistence by looking precisely at why we have to drop the original asymmetry thesis. This will refine our picture of perdurantism and contribute to the problem of the location of the whole. It is a controversial issue whether the whole object is located where its parts are. But this issue has an important impact on the question of the asymmetry between perdurance and endurance. If the whole is at the location of its parts, then no asymmetry at all arises. If it is not there, I take the asymmetry to be profound. Thus by exploring the asymmetry, we also gain insights into the question of the location of the whole. These insights might help to decide, whether it is only a part or (also) the perduring whole which is located at a certain spacetime point. Regarding the asymmetry between perdurantism and endurantism I will conclude that, since either there is no asymmetry at all or the asymmetry is so strong that the perdurantistic coexistence relation has to be very different from the endurantistic version, both cases refute the originally stated asymmetry thesis.

2. Assumptions

The previously mentioned asymmetry between endurantism and perdurantism is said to take place under the so called eternalist hypothesis. I will not challenge this, but just spell out what this means. Eternalism is often identified with the tenseless block universe view.[3] According to the block view, events exist by being located at some spacetime point p[4] or other. The block is tenseless, if there is no monadic intrinsic property of 'presentness'. The block universe view is opposed to the growing block view, according to which the present and the past are real, but future events are yet to come. So the set of existing entities grows, as time passes. It is also opposed to presentism, the doctrine that only the present is real. Past things no longer exist and future things don't exist yet.

As a second assumption Balashov restricts the analysis in this case to spatially unextended objects. This restriction avoids some difficulties with spatially extended objects, such as criss-crossing hyperplanes.[5] Furthermore, spatially unextended objects have some nice features. First of all, an invariant proper time can be ascribed. This allows at least locally for an absolute relation of earlier-later. Secondly, the triviality objection, raised by Ted Sider[6], can thereby be avoided. Sider argues that the claim that persisting objects are 'wholly present at each moment at which they exist' is either trivially true or obviously false. Siders claim crucially relies on the impossibility of gaining and losing (spatial-) parts, like fingernails or hair. Spatially unextended objects have no spatially parts by definition and thus undermine his argument.[7]

3. Balashov's Asymmetry Thesis revisited

Having made these assumptions, let us start by stating the different theories at stake. The two main candidates for a theory of persistence under the eternalist assumption are perdurantism and endurantism. Perdurantism was introduced as an answer to the old problem of change: Objects change over time (people grow, moodlights change their colour), which seems to imply that the very same object has incompatible properties at different times. But this, at least at first view, contradicts Leibniz's Law of the 'indiscernibility of identicals', which states, that if α and β are identical they must have the same properties.

The straightforward answer that those objects don't have the incompatible properties *at the same time* doesn't help. For we need a theory that shows *how* having incompatible properties at different times removes the contradiction.[8]

Perdurantism apparently tackles the problem of the indiscernibility of identical simply by denying the identity. The entities that really exemplify the properties, so it seems, are rather the temporal parts of the perduring object. Thus, no problem arises, since the temporal part that has (say) the property F is numerically different from the temporal part that has the contrary property G. So according to perdurantism the object is to be *(proper-) time-indexed.*

$$O(\tau_1) \text{ is F and } O(\tau_2) \text{ is G.}$$ [9]

But there is also an answer endurantists can give: They believe that persisting objects are not temporal extended and hence have no temporal parts. It is the object itself that has the properties. In order to avoid a conflict with Leibinz's Law, the time-index must be put somewhere else. A first move is to deny the incompatibility by (proper-) time-indexing the involved properties (indexicalism):

$$O \text{ is } F(\tau_1) \text{ and } O \text{ is } G(\tau_2).$$

But then an object that remains red all the time is conceived of as changing all the time, from being (say) red(τ1) to being red(τ11), which is counter-intuitive. To avoid this red(τ1) would have to be strictly identical to red(τ11) and all the other red(τn). But from a purely formal point of view red(τ1) and red(τ11) are just two different predicates.[10] For that reason endurantists tend to favour adverbialism, the strategy not to index the predicates themselves, but rather the having of the properties. This is done by either indexing the copula, or adding a (proper-) time-indexed adverb.

$$O \text{ is } \tau_1\text{-ly F and } O \text{ is } \tau_2\text{-ly G.}$$

This leads to the following rough characterisation of endurantism and perdurantism in spacetime. Endurantistic objects are wholly present at each τ of their career. They thus persist by being multiply located. In contrast perduring objects are only partially present at each point in spacetime and thus have temporal parts. The perduring objects *are* their worldlines and are exactly located there.[11]

To be precise here: Not only straight, but any timelike curve in spacetime could represent the worldline of an object. But still, the perduring object is the whole worldline, whereas the enduring object is at every point of the worldline wholly present, and thus multilocated.

3.1 Balashov's argument and reactions to it

By explicating the assumptions and roughly drawing the outlines of the theories to be discussed, we have everything set to go into detail. Since we are dealing with spatially unextended objects we do not run into any trouble *locally*. So it is not surprising, that we have to consider at least two objects that are (for a while) spacelike separated, and a relation between them, in this case the relation of coexistence.

Balashovs' (2000) argument against endurantism in the context of SR consists of three steps: CASS[12], the asymmetry thesis and the absurdity thesis. CASS states, that coexistence must be grounded in a relation of spacelike separation. Balashov argues that this is the only plausible account, which is symmetric, relevant and objective. He later[13] changes his opinion and presents CASH[14] as the best fitting account. Objects coexist, according to CASH, if they share a common hyperplane. To see how the original argument is supposed to work, we should stick to CASS for the moment. The main idea of this approach is that an object coexists with everything, which is spacelike separated from its location.

The second step in Balashovs argument is to claim an asymmetry between endurantism and perdurantism. First both, the endurantist and the perdurantist must accept that according to CASS an object can coexist with two objects, which are timelike separated from each other. These objects do not coexist which each other. This is common ground, according to Balashov, which both have to acknowledge. The asymmetry then arises, because the endurantist is obliged to do more. She, and only she, has to ascribe tensed determinations on top of that. Balashov puts it this way:

> It is imperative for the endurantist, but entirely meaningless for the perdurantist, to ascribe tensed determinations to the existence of other objects. (Balashov, 2000, 155)

We will come back to this soon, since this thesis will be the focus of the further analysis. Balashov's argument concludes by stating that the consequences are not bearable for the endurantist. He claims that it is absurd to ascribe tensed determinations to objects, which don't coexist with each other, because this brings them together in existence in a temporally loaded sense.

Cody Gilmore replies to this argument in 2002 with his paper 'Balashov on special relativity, coexistence and temporal parts'.[15] He calls his account of coexistence REL, because for him coexistence is relative to a hyperplane of Simultaneity. In his view, the question whether two objects coexist cannot be answered in a plain way. It is incomplete, like the expression: 'Alice is smaller than_'. To see that this is incomplete, consider the question 'Is Alice smaller than_?', which could also not be answered. Both need a second argument to make sense. So it could be truthfully said, that she is smaller than Bob. Of course the truth value depends on the object Alice is compared to. Although she is smaller than Bob, it could be wrong that Alice is smaller than Peter[16]. We can transfer these thoughts into the topic of coexistence in SR. Gilmore believes coexistence to be similar to an incomplete expression. One object O can coexist with another object O′ on a hyperplane, say HPS_1, and also not coexist with O′ on another hyperplane HPS_2. The question whether O and O′ coexist (full stop/simpliciter) cannot be answered, since coexistence itself is a relative matter.

Before we continue our main line of argument, let me raise a side-question here. Why does Gilmore talk about hyperplanes of *simultaneity*? Wouldn't it be sufficient to just talk about (maybe flat), timelike (or achronal) hyperplanes? Hyperplane dependence is Lorentz-invariant, which is a nice feature. Frame dependence cannot demand this and 'simultaneity' seems to suggest frame dependence. So one could think that it would be better to drop 'simultaneity' altogether. But, if you drop frame dependence, and just go with hyperplane dependence then the difference between Gilmores REL and Balashovs CASH mizzles off.[17]

Back to business. As we have seen, Gilmore criticises Balashov's first step, but he also attacks the other two. So he thinks that there is neither an asymmetry nor that the claims including tensed determinations are especially troublesome, or even absurd. We will accept his criticism of the absurdity thesis now, as we wish to focus on the asymmetry thesis. Gilmore's argument against the asymmetry thesis goes like this:

> Although Bob [a perduring object] is not wholly present at pB, there is a temporal part of Bob that is wholly present at pB. [. . .] The perdurantist exchanges commitments of one sort for commitments of a second sort, where those of the second sort are no less troubling than those of the first. (Gilmore, 2002, 248)

He introduces Jim, the temporal part of perduring Bob at pB and lets him do all the work Bob does, such as exemplifying properties or standing in relation to other entities. According to Gilmore, Jim would then face the same problems. In particular Jim would have to ascribe the same tensed determinations as Bob. This seems to work at first glance, but closer inspection reveals a problem. Jim is a temporal part, wholly present at pB and he is numerically different from the temporal part at pB′. This is in sharp contrast to the endurantist's account, where OE is everywhere numerically identical. Considering this, we see that there still is an asymmetry between endurantism and perdurantism.

This asymmetry falls into place, if we investigate the 'tensed determinations' involved. The ones we have to consider are: 'no longer', 'still', 'already' and 'not yet'. They all have something in common, namely that they involve two distinct (space-)timepoints. They carry information about the present moment and about some other moment, earlier or later. *Not yet* for example, tells us that something is not the case at the present moment, but will be the case at some moment later than now. It is of vital importance for this concept to include two moments. That the matter at hand is not the case at present does not suffice for, ascribing the tensed determination 'not yet' to it. Additionally, claims about some later time are needed. This lets us face the problems with Jim squarely. Temporal parts don't persist themselves and thus Jim, being a temporal part, cannot carry information about two points in time. This seems to be in line with what Ian Gibson and Oliver Pooley do, who make a concession to Balashov regarding the asymmetry thesis in their Paper 'Relativistic Persistence' from 2006.[18] They reject CASS and the absurdity thesis, but about asymmetry they write:

> It seems that Balashov is right to suggest that such locutions ['still', 'no longer'] are intimately tied to the object's being multiply located. [...] There really is an asymmetry between perduring and enduring objects [...], whilst objects may literally still or no longer exist for enduring objects, for perduring objects they may do so only in a vicarious sense. (Gibson & Pooley, 2006, 173)

They argue that this asymmetry is not enough to make Balashov's argument go through, but I think we don't even have to make this concession and we should not. By explaining why not, I hope to show that we can refine our picture of perdurantism and the amalgamation of the question of the location of the whole and the coexistence of objects in spacetime.

3.2 About 'tensed determinations'

Since tensed determinations play an important role for establishing the asymmetry in the first place, the first thing we have to do is to take a closer look at them from an eternalist point of view. Roughly, one could say, that something is tensed if it has some kind of reference to the present.[19] This is to be contrasted very sharply with a reference to an (space-)timepoint. With this distinction in mind, it seems charitable to interpret Balashov as talking about tensed determinations and not (space-)time-point-indexed determinations, or proper-time-indexed determinations. To illustrate this point, look at these two quotes from Balashov.

> "Still", "already", "no longer", and "not yet" are tensed determinations. (Balashov, 2000, 153)

> (T)emporally-laden determinations, such as *still*, *already* and the like. (Balashov, 2004, 11)

They suggest that Balashov really believes determinations like 'still' to have tensed content. And I think he is right to call them tensed, if we are talking about sentences and beliefs. Here is why: It is commonly accepted that there are tensed sentences and beliefs, although the tense can sometimes be implicit and not stated. The sentence 'E exists no longer.' means *prima facie* 'E exists *now* no longer.' The sentence 'E exists at-t no longer.' is meaningless, since 'no longer' needs a reference to the present.

I am aware that there are good reasons for tensed beliefs, such as Arthur Prior's famous Thank-goodness argument.[20] So the problem of tense is by no means restricted to tensed determinations. But, independently of any other arguments for tensed beliefs and sentences, I think that tensed determinations need tensed sentences. We have to be careful nonetheless since we want to make some ontological claims about the persistence of objects and their coexistence. By just acknowledging the tensed content of some sentence or belief, we can be still neutral in respect to ontological questions.

We have to slow down at this point and remember the eternalist assumption. We would be in trouble if tensed facts would follow from tensed determinations. But – thank goodness – they are not necessary. This was the great change from the old B-theories[21] to the NTT[22]. David Hugh Mellor in his Real Time[23] and then Real Time II[24], acknowledges tensed sentences and beliefs, but tried to show, that they are made true by B-truthmakers. This could be the way tensed determinations and eternalism go together. As this is not the topic of this paper, it does not matter if you are unhappy with Mellor's particular way of bridging the gap between tensed sentences and a tenseless eternalistic world view. I'm in no special need for a theory since the whole debate rests on the eternalisitic assumption and thereby the prerequisite of the compatibility of both endurantism and perdurantism with eternalism. There are good arguments for tensed beliefs and it is plausible to take 'still' and the like to be tensed in just that way. Mellor's account could be one way of combining this with eternalism. If this is defective, there must be another way, according to the assumption. All we have to take home is some kind of tenseless truthmakers for tensed determinations. If you do not believe in tensed beliefs then you do not have to take this detour, of course.

3.3 About 'tensed determinations' in Minkowski spacetime

I still need to analyse tensed determinations in SR. We already noted that 'still' and its companions involve two distinct moments. It's easy to see how to spell this out classically. Consider object O′ being still in existence for O at t and assume that we have absolute time in a classical context.

Object O′ exists still for O at t, iff O coexists at t with O′ and if they both coexisted earlier, say at t_1.

So much for the classical case. What is the relativistic counterpart to this? To work this out, the idea is that O′ must coexist with O at p and that there must be a p_1, which is earlier (say, in respect to the proper time of O) and on which O also coexists with O′. But look at the following situation, where O′ is everywhere spacelike separated from p:

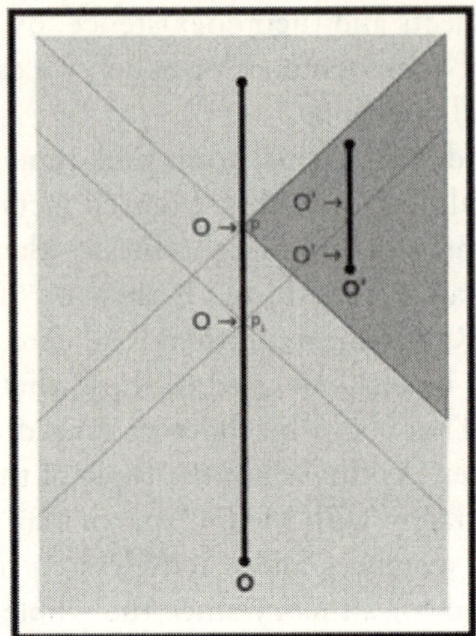

Figure 1: Spacelike separation

If so, it has neither a part in the future lightcone of p, nor in the past lightcone. According to CASS, O′ coexists with O at p, but does it still coexist? The classical analogue would be an instantaneous object, which coexists with O but clearly does not *still* coexist with O, since there is no earlier time at which they coexisted. The relativistic case is not so clear: should we restrict the truth conditions of 'O' is still in existence for O′ to those cases, where there is at least a part of O′ in the past lightcone of p? Accounts like CASS are meant to take care of this. On the other hand, there is the spacetime point p_1, which is in the absolute past of p. O exists at p_1 and coexists with O′ there, so this could be an argument that O still coexists at p with O′.

We can put this point aside for now, because the argument doesn't rely on it. Also, the problem doesn't arise for 'no longer', since this involves the idea that O′ doesn't coexist with O at p, which in turn sees to it that O′ exists in the absolute past of p. For the rest of the paper we can stick to 'no longer' and go on by looking at the truth conditions Gibson and Pooley (2006, 173) give:

O′ no longer exists for the enduring O, at p:
(a) O′ does not exist for O at p
(b) O′ does exist for O at p′ in the absolute past of p

O′ no longer exists for the perduring O, at p:
(a) O′ does not exist for a part of O at p
(b) O′ does exist for a part of O at p′ in the absolute past of p

These truth conditions are blatantly asymmetric, since the truth conditions for the perduring object contain the phrase 'a part of', which does (rightly) not appear in the endurantist version. The idea behind this seems to be a well known distinction between endurantism and perdurantism. At p, one could say, there is only the temporal part TP2 of the perduring object and at p′ there is only the TP1 of it. The enduring object on the other hand is said to be wholly present at p and at p′. So what there is at p and at p′ seems strictly identical in the endurantist case and not identical in the perdurantist case.

The affair might be a little different and to see why, we have to come back to a point, which was made at the beginning of this paper. We said that change consist in a combination of identity and difference.[25] If we think that what there is at p and at p′ is not identical in the perdurantist case then the identity over time is at stake. To turn this into a question: Where is the perduring object, if not at the location of its parts? To bother the space analogy imagine me sitting at my writing desk, putting my finger down.

What is my finger touching? The table or only a part of the table?

David Lewis writes in *The Plurality of Worlds*[26] about the different ways in which objects can be said to persist. He considers endurance, perdurance and presentism, but the neutral word for him is 'persists':

[…] something persists if it […] exists at various times. (Lewis, 1986, 202)

We are obliged by this to name an entity that exists at various times, if we want to talk about persistence at all. This entity cannot, in the perdurantist case, be one of the (temporal) parts, for they are instantaneously confined at their respective location, they themselves do not persist. We can neither say that nothing is identical through various times, because then there would be no changing object. Without identity over time, there would be just difference and hence no persistence. I take this to be an important point, since there must be a distinction between an object changing, and being exchanged (replaced by a numerical different one). It is a completely different story if a moodlight changes from red to green, or if a red light bulb is exchanged for a green one. To put this in a dramatic form: If there was no identity over time, perdurantism would not be an account of change at all.

This is the problem of strict identity, a problem the perdurantist should have something to say about. Ted Sider has something to say about this in *Four dimensionalism*[27]. He says:

> Everyone who accepts the basic phenomenon of persistence over time accepts 'strict' identity over time [. . .] three- and four-dimensionalists alike. A space-time worm with temporal parts today and tomorrow exists today, and also tomorrow. It [...] is strictly identical with itself. So it exists today and is strictly identical with something that exists tomorrow. (Sider, 2001, 54–55)

And this could be a solution to our problem! I said 'could' since I'm not convinced that it is true. But I don't need to be, since the core of my argument is this:

(P1) If Sider is right then there is no asymmetry
(P2) Sider is right
(C) There is no asymmetry

(P1) can be defended and I will argue for this in the following section. But I will remain neutral about whether P2 is true and by that whether the perduring whole is at the location of its parts. Instead I will do a case-by-case analysis and consider what follows if it is located there and what if it is not. If the latter is the case, we still learn an important lesson and to this the section 3.3.2 will be devoted.

3.3.1 OP is located at various p: no asymmetry

Let's start with the assumption that Sider is right. Then, by the very difficult logical deduction of modus ponens we can conclude, that there is no asymmetry. For the truth conditions of Gibson and Pooley this means that we can erase the 'a part of' without loss of meaning, since it is the perduring object itself that is located at p and the objects themselves are coexisting. So we get the following symmetric truth conditions:

O′ no longer exists for the enduring or perduring O, at p:
(a) O′ does not exist for O at p
(b) O′ does exist for O at p′ in the absolute past of p

The perduring object OP is identical at p with the temporal part at of OP. To strengthen this side of the case-by-case analysis we can refer to what David Lewis says, in another context:[28]

'That any two stages Si and Sj are I-related iff the corresponding continuant persons Ci and Cj are identical.' (Lewis, 1983, 60)

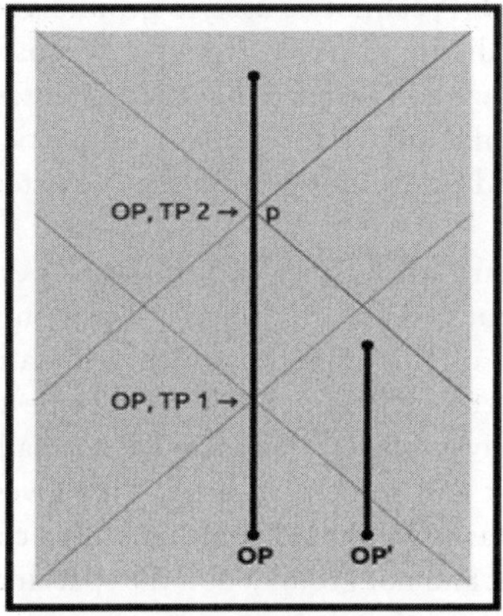

Figure 2: OP at p: Symmetric coexistence

Thus, if we are convinced, that the whole is located at the location of its parts, then this changes the situation for the perdurantist. We can apply this to the case with OP and OP′ and see that TP1 is identical-at-p with OP (TP1 $=_{p1}$ OP) and that TP2 $=_{p2}$ OP. But the really important part is that OP is located at both p1 and p2. Moreover, it is identical to itself, thus OP = OP. This is essentially like the endurantist version. So no asymmetry can be established here and we have to reject the corresponding thesis by Balashov.

To sum up, we disagree with Gibson and Pooley's concession and end up with the same result as Gilmore. But although the result is the same, we offer a completely different argument. This, however, is only the intermediate result. It depends on the assumption that Sider is right. As we do not want to judge whether this is the case or not, we still have to consider what follows if his claim is not true.

3.3.2 OP is located only wholly: serious asymmetry

In this variant of the argument we deny that an object is located at the location of its parts. What exists at p_1 is not OP, but TP1 and only TP1. If we take this seriously, we cannot ground the coexistence of two objects in the spacelike separation of p_1 and p_1'. It is undoubtedly true that a spacetime point at which OP is not located, say p_P in the absolute past of the birth of OP, cannot be used to ground a relation with OP as relatum. But what distinguishes p_P from p_1? We just agreed that OP is not located at p_1. If we don't want to be inconsistent, we must also claim that p_1 cannot ground any relation of OP. In particular, the spacelike separation of p1 and p1′ cannot ground the coexistence relation of OP and OP′.

It seems like we are stuck, since our aim was to establish an account of the relation of coexistence. But there is a way in which we can give interesting version of this relation, which also satisfies our primary goals: The coexistence relation should neither be trivial, nor empty. This means for a given object, there should normally be some objects that coexist with it and some that don't. This gives us a pretty clear description of the task: We should come up with a coexistence relation, which is contingent and not grounded in the spacelike separation of the locations of the parts of the perduring object.

To solve this task we just have to consider why we could want to reject Sider's identity thesis. We could deny the existence of OP at p_1, because it is not the whole object (OP) that is at p_1, but only a (temporal) part of it. Then, if we are interested in a relation between two objects and not their parts, we should consider them. Here is my proposal for a coexistence relation:

(SA) Given a perduring object, everything coexists with it, except objects or events entirely located in the absolute future of its end or in the absolute past of its beginning.

To get a better grasp on this relation, we can look at some of its features. The first thing which is notable is that the set of coexisting objects does not vary with different τ. Consider three objects OP, OP′ and OP″, with OP″ in the absolute future of OP′. If we also assume that both OP′ and OP″ lie in the area specified by (SA), concerning OP, we can only say that OP coexists with OP′ and OP coexists with OP″. We are not entitled to say anything more. On this view it would be meaningless to

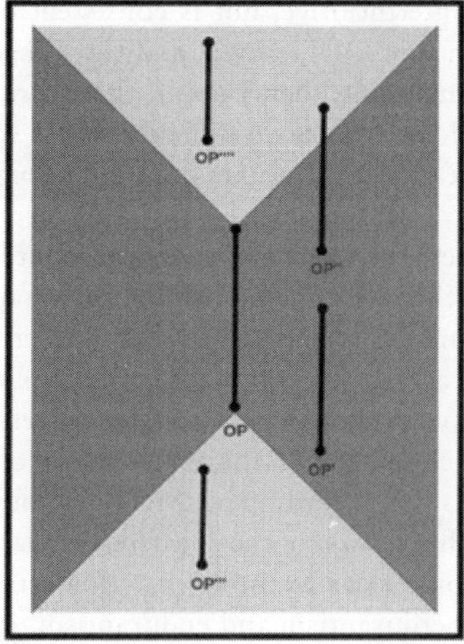

Figure 3: (SA)-Coexistence

say OP coexists with OP′ at τ_1. There is no room for a (proper-) time-relativation.

This is the great problem of this account of coexistence. OP coexists *simpliciter* with OP′ and with OP″, while they do not coexist simpilciter. This relation is clearly not transitive. But there is a pre-theoretical concept of coexistence, which is also not transitive. If my grandfather died before I was born, there is a sense, in which my father coexists with him and with me, although I never coexist with my grandfather. I do not want to argue for this view, I just want to mention the analogy to the pre-theoretical concept of coexistence. The main idea of this paper is not to convince anybody to adopt a certain position, but rather a hypothetical approach. I want to show the costs of adopting a certain view, by showing its consequences. And I take it to follow directly from denying the existence of OP at some p that coexistence has to be something like (SA). The real cost for coexistence à la (SA) is, that it is not timely in any sense. Even in the eternalist picture, we have space for some 'dynamics', namely the variation of what exists at different spacetime-points/τ. But (SA)-coexistence does not vary with different τ, it is a simple yes/no choice: Either two objects coexist, or they do not.[29]

This may seem counterintuitive, but is consistent on a closer look. If we deny the existence of OP at any p, and the τ change from spacetime point to spacetime point, then I doubt that there is room for the aforesaid dynamics. If the objects do not exist at the spacetime points, then what exists at the spacetime points does not *change* with different spacetime points.[30]

After discussing where the trouble with this account lies, we still have to consider if it solves the task of being neither universal nor empty. OP′ and OP″ are some examples for objects, which coexist with OP, so one part is already taken care of. They grant that the coexistence relation is not empty.[31] All we have to show is that it is not universal. But just consider OP‴, which lies completely in the absolute past of OP, or OP⁗ in the absolute future. As OP according to (SA) does coexist neither with OP‴ nor with OP⁗, this version of the coexistence relation is not trivial.

It should have become clear by now, that this establishes a strong asymmetry between perdurantism and endurantism. It is a key feature of endurantism that objects exist *at* their respective various p, this is the very idea of multi-location. As we disagreed on this basic level for perduring objects, we had to give a completely different coexistence relation for them.[32] This closes the second part of our case-by-case analysis. We have seen the possibility to be convinced that the perduring whole is not at the location of its parts and still come up with a coexistence relation, which satisfies the task. We have approached the problems with this relation.

4. Conclusion

Either the perduring whole is at the location of its parts or it is located only wholly. It may be controversial which of these options is true, but one of them has to be. We considered both options hypothetically without taking a stand on which is correct and in both cases the purported asymmetry could not be stated, not even in a vicarious sense.

If OP is located at (various) p then there is no asymmetry at all. However, if OP is only located wholly and hence not at (various) p, then the asymmetry is much worse than expected, which is visible in the (SA)-coexistence relation. This relation is not only not transitive, but also not timely in any sense.

Notes

I would like to thank the participators of the *Temporal Existence and Persistence in Spacetime* workshop for the stimulating discussions, especially Yuri Balashov, Cody Gilmore and Oliver Pooley. Also I am very grateful for the participants of the colloquium of Prof. Bartels and Prof. Brendel and the audience at the *SOPHiA* conference for their comments on an earlier draft of this paper. Special gratitude belongs doubtless to Cord Friebe, with whom I could discuss the paper in detail and who always helped me with constructive criticism. Caro Haupt, Stefan Heidl, Thomas Müller, Thorben Petersen and Emanuel Viebahn provided me with orthographical as well as with substantial insights.

1 The considered accounts of persistence will be endurance and perdurance. Exdurance (See (Sider, 2001, section 5.8) does not play a role in my argument, but I cannot see how this variant of 4-dimensionalism could bypass it.

2 See (Gilmore, 2002) and (Gibson & Pooley, 2006, 167–177).

3 For a detailed analysis of the relation between eternalism and the block universe view see (Friebe, 2011) in this volume. For now, I will ignore the arguments given there against the identification of the two, although I find them convincing.

4 I will talk about spacetime points p, instead of time points t, which are not available in the geometric Minkowski interpretation of the Special Theory of Relativity (SR).

5 See (Gilmore, 2006).

6 See (Sider, 2001) page 64.

7 In particular Sider argues that it is trivially true that the object has every part that it now has now and it is obviously false that all the parts that the considered object ever has are present at each (proper-) time of its existence. Spatial unextended objects undermine the either-or-structure of Siders argument, since their impossibility of gaining and losing parts is independent of the theory of persistence we choose and thus independent of the 'wholly present' in the endurantist case.

8 See (Lewis, 1986) p 202.

9 '$O(\tau_1)$' and '$O(\tau_2)$' refer to two different temporal parts of the persisting object O.

10 It is possible, however, to add some structure to the realm of predicates, say by adding axioms, or by some second order structure, which seems to be more comfortable, but anyhow, this structure does not follow directly. Without it the predicate 'red(τ1)' is as similar to 'red(τ11)' as to 'unicorn'.

11 This formulation depends on the thesis of supersubstantivalism (the identity of material objects and the regions of spacetime they occupy), which is widely but not universally accepted. So it is possible to be perdurantist without being a supersubstantivalism. Nevertheless this is only important for the formulation; the contrast to endurantism remains intact.

12 Coexistence as spacelike separation.

13 See (Balashov, 2005) and (Balashov, 2011).
14 Coexistence as sharing hyperplane.
15 See (Gilmore, 2002).
16 Since nobody is smaller than Peter Maffay.
17 To illustrate this point, consider transitivity. Balashov describes CASH as the "n-place relation of belonging to a single HPS" (Balashov, 2005, 15). All objects belonging to one HPS establish a equivalence relation. This is transitive in the sense that if O1 and O2 belong a given hyperplane HPS1 and O2 and O3 also belong to HPS1, then O1 and O3 belong to HPS1. This may seem a nonstandard form of transitivity, but it is the same way in which REL is transitive: "REL makes coexistence a transitive relation, in the sense that for any objects A, B, and C, and any plane t, if A coexists at t with B, and B coexists at t with C, then A coexists at t with C." (Gilmore, 2002, 15)
18 See (Gibson & Pooley, 2006).
19 'Something' should be understood as widely as possible, including sentences and determinations.
20 (Prior,1976).
21 Old B-theorists include Gottlob Frege and Bertrand Russell. Take, for example, this quote from Russell: 'Change is the difference, in respect of truth or falsehood, between a proposition concerning and entity and the time T, and a proposition concerning the same entity and the time T*, provided that these propositions differ only by the fact that T occurs in the one where T* occurs in the other.' (Russell,1937, 469)
22 New Tensless Theory of time.
23 (Mellor, 1981).
24 (Mellor, 1998).
25 Consider the following quotes: 'change needs identity as well as difference' (Mellor, 1998, p 89) and 'What is change? [...] change consists in an object (the substratum) having first one attribute, then another attribute contrary to the first.' (Simons, 1991, 131)
26 (Lewis, 1986).
27 (Sider, 2001).
28 (Lewis, 1983).
29 We can safely talk like this, since the coexistence relation is symmetric according to (SA). So if A coexists with B, than B also coexists with A, or more simple: A and B coexist.
30 Of course, there are different parts instantiated at different spacetime points, but these are confined to these locations. And as each of them doesn't persist, nothing changes and thus no talk of dynamic is justified.
31 To be precise here: Their possibility grants, that the relation is not necessary empty.
32 Even if it's possible for the endurantist to also adopt a principle like (SA), the asymmetry remains, since the perdurantist is forced, whereas the endurantist may chose.

Bibliography

Balashov, Yuri, 2000b: Enduring and Perduring Objects in Minkowski Spacetime. In: *Philosophical Studies* 99, pp. 129–166.

Balashov, Yuri, 2005: Special relativity, Coexistence and Temporal Parts: A Reply to Gilmore. In: *Philosophical Studies* 124, pp. 1–40.

Balashov, Yuri, 2010: *Persistence in Spacetime.* Oxford: Oxford University Press.

Frege, Gottlob, 1892: On Sense and Meaning. In: Peter Geach and Max Black (eds.): *Translations from the Philosophical Writings of Gottlob Frege*, Third Edition, Totowa, NJ: Barnes and Noble Books.

Friebe, Cord, 2011: Eternalism and the Temporal Content of Persistence. In: Philosophia Naturalis.

Gibson, Ian & Pooley, Oliver, 2006: Relativistic Persistence. In: *Philosophical Perspectives,* 20: *Metaphysics*. Blackwell: Malden, pp 157–198.

Gilmore, Cody, 2002: Balashov on Special Relativity, Coexistence, and Temporal Parts. In: *Philosophical Studies* 109, pp. 241–263.

Gilmore, Cody S., 2006: Where in the relativistic world are we? In: Philosophical Perspectives, 20: *Metaphysics*. Malden: Blackwell, pp. 199–236.

Lewis, David, 1976: Survival and Identity. In: *Philosophical Papers, Vol. 1.* 1983, Oxford: Oxford University Press, pp. 55–77.

Lewis, David, 1986: *On the Plurality of Worlds*, Oxford: Blackwell Publishers.

Mellor, David Hugh, 1981: *Real Time I.* Cambridge: Cambridge University Press.

Mellor, David Hugh, 1998: *Real Time II.* New York: Routledge.

Prior, Arthur N., 1959: Thank goodness that's over. In: *Philosophy,* 34, pp. 12–17.

Russell, Bertrand, 1903: *The Principles of Mathematics.* Michigan: University of Michigan Press.

Sider, Theodore, 2003: *Four-Dimensionalism: An Ontology of Persistence and Time,* Oxford: Oxford University Press.

Simons, Peter, 1991: On Being Spread out in Time: Temporal Parts and the Problem of Change. In: W. Spohn, B. C. van Fraassen, and B. Skyrms, *Existence and Explanation*. Dodrecht: Kluwer.

Cord Friebe

Eternalism and the Temporal Content of Persistence

Abstract

The concept of "eternalism" or the "block view" is ambiguous if applied to spacetime theories: a tenseless but temporal view, on the one hand, has to be distinguished from a timeless one, on the other. In the first part I will spell out this difference. The second part presupposes the (more promising) temporal tenseless block universe view and argues that perdurantism is, on this basis, as 'dynamical' as endurantism. So, if we are after a temporal reading of eternalism and if we intend to keep alive the temporal content of persistence, both variants, eternalistic endurance/perdurance, are equally (in)appropriate for SR.

Zusammenfassung

In Anwendung auf Raumzeit-Theorien ist der Eternalismus bzw. die Auffassung der Raumzeit als Block-Universum zweideutig: Eine bloß tempuslose, aber temporale Lesart ist von einer zeitlosen zu unterscheiden. Dies geschieht im ersten Teil des vorliegenden Aufsatzes. Im zweiten wird die interessantere, temporale Interpretation zugrunde gelegt und gezeigt, dass auf dieser Basis der Perdurantismus ebenso 'dynamisch' ist wie der Endurantismus. Versteht man daher "Eternalismus" temporal und hält also am zeitlichen Gehalt von "Persistenz" fest, erweisen sich beide Varianten, eternalistische Enduranz/Perduranz, als der SRT gleichermaßen (un)angemessen.

The metaphysics of persistence and the problem of change have recently attracted philosophers of spacetime physics. The intuition is that relativity, especially special relativity (SR), confronts them with peculiar difficulties, challenges certain views like endurantism, and adds fruitful aspects to the debate. I am in doubt on that: I intend to argue that, given eternalism, the different views of persistence and change are on a par for Minkowski spacetime. The problem, however, is that the concept of "eternalism" or the "block view" is ambiguous if applied to spacetime theories: there are, I think, essentially two different views of the block universe; a tenseless but temporal view on the one hand and a timeless one on the other. In the first part I will spell out this difference. The second part presupposes the temporal tenseless block universe view and argues with this underlying eternalist hypothesis that perdurantism is as 'dynamical' as endurantism and therefore equally adequate (or, of course, equally inappropriate) for SR. So, in fact, it is only argued that, given the temporal block universe view, the different views of persistence and change are on a par, but I strongly suggest that this is the more interesting view. Therefore the timeless view is out of consideration in the second part of the paper.

In the debate it is usually assumed:

1) Concerning *Neo-Newtonian* spacetime all views of persistence and change discussed in analytic philosophy are equally well reformulatable and equally adequate. So, the triviality objection (see Sider, 2001, 64), paradoxes of multi-location (see Barker/Dowe, 2003), and problems with fusion and fission offer no decisive arguments against endurantism; if there are any they stem from Minkowski spacetime.

2) All views of persistence and change are *empirically* compatible with SR. There are no physical grounds in the experimental sense of physics favoring one view over its rival(s)[1]. It is rather the *geometry* of Minkowski spacetime, or its philosophical interpretation, that could have ontological commitments that until now are overseen by analytic philosophers.

3) And the reason for that is *not* that the geometry of Minkowski spacetime commits us to the eternalist view of temporal existence. Endurantism and perdurantism are equally adequate for Neo-Newtonian spacetime but not *in virtue of* the fact that that spacetime is also compatible with several other views of temporal existence, like presentism or growing block. Endurantism and perdurantism are both compatible with eternalism.[2]

But if all that is assumed it seems, at least at first view, to be surprising that SR should provoke an interesting debate about persistence. For a skeptic could argue that:

1) The essential difference is that Neo-Newtonian spacetime, even if interpreted eternalistically, is temporally separated, while Minkowski spacetime is not. The latter, in contrast to the former, is not only *formulatable* as a 4-D spacetime theory, but it is *necessarily* a 4-D spacetime

theory. So, it is obviously in conflict with a view according to which the ontologically basic objects are 3-D, as the endurantist would have it. And it is overwhelmingly more natural that physical objects are fundamentally 4-D. Hence, perdurantism is favored by SR from the beginning.

2) Since the geometrical structure of Minkowski spacetime implies many problems with "extension"[3], it is overwhelmingly more natural that the fundamental physical objects are point-events. The only requirement for composing those point-events to extended wholes is *empirical adequateness*. So, if the intended compositions are empirically indistinguishable, as it is assumed, their differences are ontologically irrelevant. Endurance and perdurance are on a par, since the composing of enduring or perduring objects out of fundamental point-events is merely *pragmatic*.

We have thus seemingly only two options: Either the fundamental objects are 4-D – and then perdurantism is trivially favored – or the fundamental entities are point-events – and then the endurance/perdurance distinction is ontologically irrelevant. The debate, however, is *not* going that way. But why not?

1. The eternalist hypothesis reconsidered

One of the main intuitions that motivate the debate is the idea that endurantism is more 'dynamical' than perdurantism and that such a 'dynamic' is, somehow, in conflict with SR.[4] Enduring objects *change their positions in spacetime* and have *changing relations to other objects*, it is said (see Balashov, 2000b, 162; 2005, 15), while the perduring objects are rather "atemporally confined to their locations in spacetime" (ibid.) – even if we presuppose the same eternalist hypothesis in both cases: I would argue with that. The eternalist hypothesis is ambiguous, and *that* is where the trouble comes from. The contemporary standard B-theory of time – namely the so-called "new tenseless theory of time" (NTT; see Mellor, 1981) – has, I think, essentially *two different* reformulations for spacetime theories.[5] Its usual characterization by (so-called) past, present, and future entities being all equally real and by denying anything instantiating A-properties like presentness or pastness is *incomplete*. For this is only a characterization in a *general* sense. There is a *further* characteristic that distinguishes two specifically different block universe views – namely an objective, not only pragmatic, *temporally restricted* sense of existence that a block universe may allow for, or not.[6]

To repeat the problem, let us look at the following claim by Mauro Dorato:

[E]ven though it is *always* true to assert that 'F occurs at t_F', such an eternal *truth* about event F in no way implies the *eternal existence* of the event F. (Dorato, 2006, 562)

The eternalist's claim that all events exist independently of being present should not mean, Dorato reminds, that each event exists at all times.[7] So far, so good: But how should one reformulate that sentence for spacetime theories? Taking into account that the primitive concept for spacetime theories is "being located at p", one could suggest the following translation:

Even though it is *always* true to assert that 'F occurs at p_F', such an eternal *truth* about event F in no way implies the *eternal existence* of the event F.

This claim, however, has a *trivial* meaning, namely that not even according to the block view an event is located at *every* p. Dorato's opponent would be a straw man, since nobody has ever argued for the absurd view that all events in spacetime are located at all p. And from that triviality it certainly does not follow that event F, located at some single p, does not exist eternally, since it *would* exist eternally if there were no moments of B-time in spacetime, like (probably) in the Gödel universe.

A second, alternative translation is the following:

Even though it is *always* true to assert that 'e occurs at frame time t^F_e', such an eternal *truth* about event e in no way implies the *eternal existence* of the event e.

Thus, although located somewhere in the block, event e exists only at a particular frame time t^F_e and, hence, not eternally, i.e., not at all those times. But this non-eternal existence at a certain time can be considered as only being a matter of convenience; the temporal restriction of existence seems to be merely pragmatic. That's *not* what the NTT usually says, for which reason relativity is, at first view, a challenge for classical B-theories of time.[8]

To continue, consider Dorato's definition of "tenseless existence":

Def: Tenseless Existence: For all present moments, event e 'exists' in a *tenseless* sense of 'existence' iff it has existed, exists in the present or will exist. (Dorato, 2006, 561)

Translated, once again, for spacetime theories "tenseless existence", as defined above, seems to be equivalent to the following definition:

Def: Event e exists in a tenseless sense of "existence" iff it is located at some spacetime point p or other (or, concerning extended objects, at some spacelike region or other).

But, while the original definition implies a temporal restriction for e occurring at a particular time (now, or in the past, or in the future), the translated version does not: being located at a particular p, for itself, tells nothing about the moment of B-time at which e exists. So, in order to make explicit what "tenseless existence" implies, one should consider Dorato's definition as a definition for a *non-perspectival* sense of "existence" which is to be contrasted with a *perspectival* one so that non-perspectival existence is an inclusion of all the different perspectival ways of being. Thus tenseless existence-*simpliciter* is to be distinguished from a *second eternalist*, likewise tenseless sense of "existence", namely existence-at-t:[9]

Def: Tenseless Existence [*at t*]: Event e exists in a tenseless (but) *perspectival* sense, i.e., relative to a given time t, iff it is located at that time (independently of t being present).

The problem then is to find the right reformulation of that definition for spacetime theories, since there the primitive concept is not "being located at t" but "being located at p". Hence, the seemingly straightforward reformulation is inappropriate:

Def: Tenseless Existence [*at p*]: Event e exists in a tenseless (but) *perspectival* sense, i.e., at a given spacetime point p, iff it is located at that p (independently of p being present).

It is inappropriate, since this restriction is trivial and not a temporal one. With that perspectival sense of "existence" not even Neo-Newtonian spacetime could express what the NTT says. Therefore "existence-at-t" transforms to "existence-*with-respect-to*-p".

Then, concerning the *Neo-Newtonian* case, one can proceed as follows:

Def (Newton 1): Tenseless Existence [*simpliciter*]: Event e exists in a *non-perspectival* sense of "existence" iff it is located at some spacetime point p or other (i.e., somewhere in spacetime).

Def (Newton 2): Tenseless Existence [*with respect to p*]: Event e exists in a *perspectival* sense of "existence", i.e., tenselessly (but) with respect to a given p, iff it is located at p or at some p′ simultaneous with p.[10]

"Newton 2" is an objective, not only pragmatic, restriction of "Newton 1" which mirrors temporal succession in the B-theoretical sense (i.e., different times are different in the sense of earlier or later).[11] These definitions reflect the ideas of NTT, namely that, first, although the sentence "e exists *simpliciter*" does *not* vary in truthvalue, e does not exist at *all* times (i.e., not with respect to *all* p), and, second, although the sentence "e exists *now*" differs in truthvalue from time to time,[12] e does not exist in dependency of being present. The new B-theorists have to fit together both aspects into the same tenseless world which requires (for spacetime theories), as we have seen, two different concepts of "tenseless existence" – the unrestricted "*simpliciter*" and the temporally restricted one.

Relativistic spacetimes with *cosmic times* could be considered as being *eternalistic* in that same sense:

Def. (cosmic time universes 1): Tenseless Existence [*simpliciter*]: Event e exists in a *non-perspectival* sense of "existence" iff it is located at some spacetime point p or other.

Def. (cosmic time universes 2): Tenseless Existence [*with respect to p*]: Event e exists in a *perspectival* sense of "existence", i.e., tenselessly (but) with respect to given p, iff it is located at that p or at some p′ that belongs to the same privileged maximal hypersurface as p, where a maximal hypersurface is privileged iff the energy-matter density is isotropic and homogeneous.[13]

But, now, what about Minkowski spacetime that contains no global invariant moment of B-time? Does a temporally not separated spacetime allow for an objective temporally restricted sense of "existence"? Putnam's classical argument turns out, in this line of interpretation, as being a challenge for standard *eternalism* – and not (or, not primarily), as it was intended, as a challenge for presentism. For according to Putnam "future things are *already* real" (Putnam, 1967, 243; italics mine), which means[14] that *with respect to a given spacetime-point p* [and not only: *simpliciter*] *all* events in spacetime are realized. There is no temporally restricted sense of "existence" if Putnam is right, i.e., existence-*simpliciter* is *co-extensive* with existence-with-respect-to-p:

Def (Putnam): Tenseless Existence: Event e exists with respect to a given spacetime point p iff it is located at p or at some p′ or other (somewhere in spacetime).

In fact, Putnam's claim that the realization relation – pRe: e is realized with respect to p – is *universal* implies that the sentence "pRe" (with e fixed) is (eternally) true for all instances of p if it is (eternally) true for any instance of p.[15] If e is realized with respect to some particular p it is realized with respect to all the other p, too: a fact that has no counterpart in traditional B-theories. Putnam's block universe is therefore not only *tense*less but in a specific sense rather *time*less,[16] namely in the way that it contains no objective perspectival sense of "existence", apparently constitutive for the concept of a "moment of B-time" in spacetime-reformulations of NTT.

Confronting analytic philosophy of time with philosophy of spacetime physics leads, therefore, to a certain confusion about the concepts of "eternalism" and "block universe" that can be resolved in the following way: One starts with a *general* meaning of the *block universe view*, characterized by the non-perspectival sense of "existence" according to which events exist by being located at some spacetime point p or other, independently of being present. On *that* level the block universe view is opposed to *dynamic* views of temporal existence, namely opposed to the *growing block view* and to *presentism*, characterized by the idea that what exists in a non-perspectival sense (i.e., *simpliciter*) *varies*, somehow, with time. But then we have to distinguish further levels of the block universe view: firstly, there are two types of block universes, specifically distinguished by being *tensed* (not yet mentioned) or *tenseless*. According to the tensed view all events exist independently of being present – at some p or other (according to the general sense) –, but there is an objective monadic property of presentness moving, somehow, on spacetime. This view corresponds to the *moving spotlight view*, i.e., it is the spacetime variant of a *static* A-theory.[17] A *tenseless* block universe, in contrast, is characterized, once again, by the idea that all events exist independently of being present, located at some p or other, but furthermore by the denial of any objective sense of "being present". The present is not only irrelevant for existence, but it lacks any objectivity whatsoever (first *differentia specifica*). Secondly, and more important for my purposes, there is still another level for block universe views: there are tenseless block universes, like Neo-Newtonian spacetime or general relativistic spacetimes with cosmic time, that are *temporally restrictable* the way that there is a likewise objective and likewise tenseless but perspectival sense of "existence", namely existence-with-respect-to-p. These views I would call "temporal tenseless block universe views". Finally, there is a tenseless block universe view according to which all events do not only exist independently of being present (general sense) and not only without any objective property of presentness (first *differentia specifica*) but furthermore independently of any spacetime point p with respect to which existence could be objectively restricted (second *differentia specifica*). Such a universe is not merely tenseless but rather "timeless", as I would call it. This is Putnam's block universe view which is hence a very specific form located on a very specific level. On *that* level it is *not* opposed to presentism or growing block, but it is rather opposed to the *temporal tenseless block universes*, i.e., to the spacetime-reformulations of NTT.

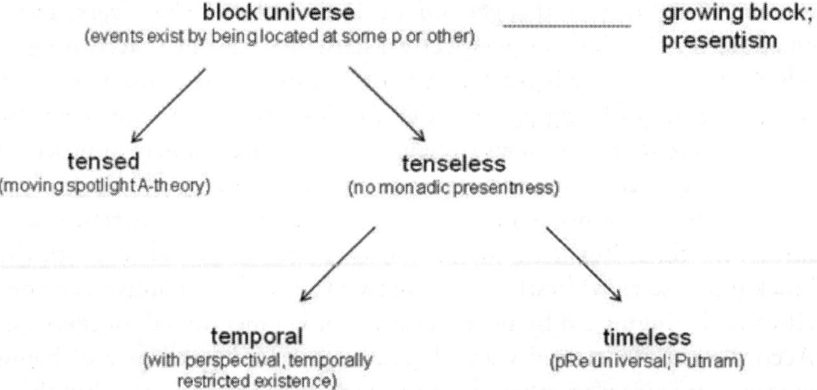

Fig. 1: Temporal existence in spacetime: different meanings of the "block universe view".

So far, so bad for SR, since up to this point Minkowski spacetime seems to represent a *timeless* universe. But the Putnam/Stein-controversy (1967/68) has opened, in this line of reasoning, a temporal reading of SR, namely a block universe view that I would call "point eternalism", characterized as follows:

Def (point-eternalism 1): Tenseless Existence [*simpliciter*]: Event e exists in a *non-perspectival* sense of "existence" iff it is located somewhere in spacetime.

Def (point-eternalism 2): Tenseless Existence [*with respect to p*]: Event e exists in a *perspectival* sense of "existence", namely tenselessly (but) with respect to a given p, iff it is located at p.

Some remarks: a) "Point eternalism 2" is not to be confounded with "tenseless existence [*at p*]", mentioned above; while it is trivial that only the event that is located at p exists *at* p, it turns out to be a substantial claim that only the event that is located at p exists *with respect to* p. b) "Point eternalism 2" is an objective, not only pragmatic, restriction of the general sense of "existence", since in accordance with Minkowski spacetime the (transitive) realization relation R could be such that the sentence "pRe" (with e fixed) is (eternally) true only for one single instance of p, namely for p_e, where e is located. c) The restriction is interpretable as a *temporal* one, taking into account that along a given worldline spacetime points could be ordered by the earlier-later relation.

Point eternalism differs essentially from Putnam's view in the following way: consider a worldline with e located at p and e′ located at p′. According to *both* views e and e′ exist in the (tenseless) *non-perspectival* sense, and p and p′ are timelike separated – that latter point is simply a fact of the mathematical/physical theory. But then it is disputable whether e′, located at p′, exists with respect to e (or p), given e at p. And, *vice versa*, it is controversial whether e exists with respect to e′ (or p′), given e′ at p′. If one argues affirmatively, namely in line with Putnam, that all events exist in the same way, one states that there is no moment of B-time and that p′ is neither earlier nor later than p (although timelike separated from p, i.e., "timelike" has, in this case, no temporal content). If one argues contrariwise, so loosely in line with Stein, that each event exists in its own perspectival way, one holds the converse view that there are many spatially unextended moments of B-time (*proper times*) and that p′ is objectively earlier or later than p. So, there is *at least one* version of a temporal tenseless block universe view in accordance with Minkowski spacetime and, perhaps, there are also other alternatives than this (counter-intuitive) point eternalism.

Now, my impression is that during the debate on *persistence* authors are switching between different block universe views. For example: when Yuri Balashov (2000b; 2005) is after an "interesting co-existence relation" between two (or more) persisting (but) spatially unextended objects, then he has mind, at least as I would read him, that in addition to the *general* sense of "existence" a temporally restricted but likewise objective sense of "existence" is needed, namely:[19]

Def (Balashov 2): Tenseless Existence [*with respect to p*]: Object o exists in a *perspectival* sense of "existence", namely tenselessly (but) with respect to a given p, iff it is located at p or at some p′ spacelike separated from p (corresponds to CASS).[20]

He is apparently operating on the "*temporal* tenseless block universe view". But certain formulations suggest otherwise: for the endurantists, he claims, the perspectival sense of existence is combined with "tensed determinations" like "already", "no longer", and so on (see Balashov, 2000b, 153), *as if* the endurantists were acting on a "*tensed* block universe view". Perduring objects, on the other hand, are described by having a "4-D shape" that is "pre-existing" or ontologically prior (Balashov, 2000a, 333), *as if* the perdurantists were operating on the "*timeless* block universe view".

Cody Gilmore (2002) argues for REL in contrast to CASS, which means to state, at least as I would read him, that the temporal restriction of existence has to be frame-dependent. Interpreted that way, he argues that frame-dependency, although not "objective" in the sense of "invariant", is harmless, because it is only the perspectival sense of "existence" that is so dependent, while the general sense is not:

> Thus, even if it is a relative matter whether Aristotle *coexists* with you [i.e., whether Aristotle tenselessly exists in the perspectival sense], it remains a non-relative, objective fact that Aristotle *exists* [i.e., that Aristotle exists *simpliciter* by being located at some p or other]. (Gilmore, 2002, 254/255)[21]

Here Gilmore apparently assumes the "*temporal* tenseless block universe view". But, then (see Gilmore, 2006, sec. 4.1) he requires for the three-dimensional enduring object (and for the three-dimensional *parts* of a perduring one) *only* "maximal achronal" (i.e., maximal spacelike) hypersurfaces that need *not* to be flat, and also Ian Gibson and Oliver Pooley (2006) stress several times that *flatness* is not needed. Since *non-flat* spacelike regions in Minkowski spacetime are *not* related with any moment of B-time, this view seems to be more natural if we presuppose *Putnam's* block universe view. Because according to that view the distinction between "timelike" and "spacelike" is all there is; any further criterion like "flatness" is unmotivated from *that* underlying eternalist hypothesis.

Balashov (2008), in contrast, argues *for* "flatness". He apparently has in mind that "spacelike" as opposed to "timelike" is *not* sufficient in order to give a complete description of the regions being exactly occupied by an enduring object (or partially by a perduring one). We need an *additional* criterion in order to preserve the *temporal* content of persistence, according to Balashov (apparently). This, however, seems to be natural only within a *temporal* tenseless block universe. Consequently, the eternalist hypothesis that underlies the debate on persistence needs a specification.

2. On the 'dynamics' of perdurance

One of the main intuitions connected with the endurance/perdurance distinction is surely that endurantism is, in some way, temporally more 'dynamical' than perdurantism and one of the most discussed arguments in favor of perdurantism is that SR cannot give any room for such an endurantist 'dynamics'. In this second part I want to sketch some points to defend the following thesis: *if* we presuppose eternalism in the sense of the *temporal* tenseless block universe view, perdurantism is *no less* 'dynamical' than endurantism.[22] So, I want to argue against Balashov's "Asymmetry Thesis", in line with Gilmore (2002) but with different arguments, which might also clarify some misunderstandings about perdurantism.

The first point to be sketched concerns the so-called *location problem*: presupposing eternalism, enduring objects are conceived of as being "multiply located" in spacetime,[23] while perduring objects are only "singly located" in spacetime (see Gilmore, 2006, and Balashov, 2008, for precise formulations). But what does "being multi-located" mean other than "to exist at various times", i.e., to exist at various proper-times, frame-times, or at various flat spacelike-regions? Interpreted this way, however, "endurance" would be the *only* sense of "persistence", since the neutral sense for eternalist persistence is precisely "to exist at various times" (according to Lewis, 1986, 202). Correspondingly, "being singly located" is not a specific characterization for perdurantism, since *instantaneous* events are also singly located in spacetime. In virtue of being instantaneous, they in principle could not exist at various times (i.e., proper-times etc.) and, *therefore,* they are singly located for which reason "being singly located" has, at first view, the meaning of "to exist only once". What then does it mean that the perduring whole is singly located in spacetime if *not* that it does *not* persist?[24] Of course, one might object, in line with Gilmore (2006, 204), that *for spacetime theories* the neutral sense of "persistence" is not "to exist at various times" but rather "having a path that is not achronal", i.e., occupying a region with timelike extension. The risk, however, is falling back into the *timeless* block universe view according to which the perduring whole exists unrestrictedly at some path or other without any temporally restricted, perspectival way of being. From the perspective of the *temporal* tenseless block universe view, it seems to be unnatural to assume that the perduring whole is singly located.

A second, alternative reading would seemingly be that the enduring object has a peculiar *property* of "being multi-located", while the perduring whole lacks that property. But the enduring object has either *time-indexed* properties[25] – according to the indexicalist version of endurantism – or it has properties in a *time-indexed way* (according to adverbialism).[26] The property of "being multi-located", however, is neither time-indexed nor could an enduring object be t-ly multi-located. Hence, it could not have that property at all (I would say[27]).

Furthermore, and independent from the specification of the block view, I think that in order to distinguish perdurantism from endurantism it is completely *irrelevant* to claim that the perduring *whole* is singly located. One could (and should) say that also the perduring object is multiply located in spacetime (i.e., that it persists by existing 'at various times') but in the way that it *has* (as opposed to that it *is*) something that is in fact singly located – namely its instantaneous temporal parts. In contrast, the enduring object neither is singly located nor has something that is singly located.

Second point (properties *simpliciter* vs. properties *at times*): sometimes it is said that perduring objects considered wholly have properties *simpliciter*, namely 4-D shapes (see Balashov, 2000a, 333), while in contrast enduring objects "instantiate a property *only* relative to a time" (Gibson/Pooley, 2006, 164; italics mine). But, that is far from being clear: what is in fact intelligible, is that each *instantaneous* temporal part of a perduring object has its (intrinsic) properties *simpliciter*, since in virtue of being instantaneous it *cannot* have them "at times". The perduring *whole*, however, *has* properties at times; it is red at t_1 (so, red at a certain proper time, a certain frame-time, or within a certain flat spacelike region) and green at t_2 – in virtue of numerically different temporal parts that are red *simpliciter* and green *simpliciter*, respectively. And it is completely irrelevant (and misleading) to state that the perduring whole would have additional properties *simpliciter* – like being multi-colored –, in order to distinguish perdurantism from endurantism. *All* persisting and changeable objects have properties *only* relative to times (i.e., proper-times etc.), one could claim, *but* in different ways: perduring objects by means of their temporal parts and enduring ones by having time-indexed-properties (indexicalism) or properties in a time-indexed way (adverbialism).[28]

By 'spatialization', the spacetime diagram representing such a situation might be mileading:

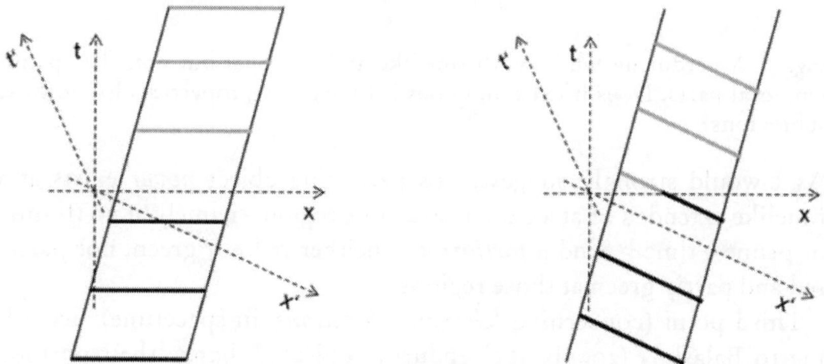

Fig. 2: A perduring object with different color-properties at different frame- and prime times. Is it multi-colored, *simpliciter*, considered wholly?

Contrary to what the representation suggests, the represented perduring object is *multiply* located in spacetime, namely at frame times t_i *and* at prime times t'_j – by having temporal parts that are singly located there. It is red *at* some frame times and green *at* some other frame times, and it is even (spatially) partly green and partly red *at* some prime times – by means of its temporal parts that have those (non-time-indexed) properties *simpliciter*. Nothing commits one to claim that it is, as a whole, singly located in spacetime and that it is, as whole, multi-colored (*simpliciter*). Doing so, is rather misleading, since then it would also be natural – unless one denies *every* perspectival way of being – to claim that it exists and has properties also at many non-achronal or achronal but non-flat subregions. For every such region would be a spatio-temporal part of the perduring whole, ontologically on a par with all the other parts, if we conceived of the whole as being singly located in spacetime and having 4D-properties *simpliciter*:

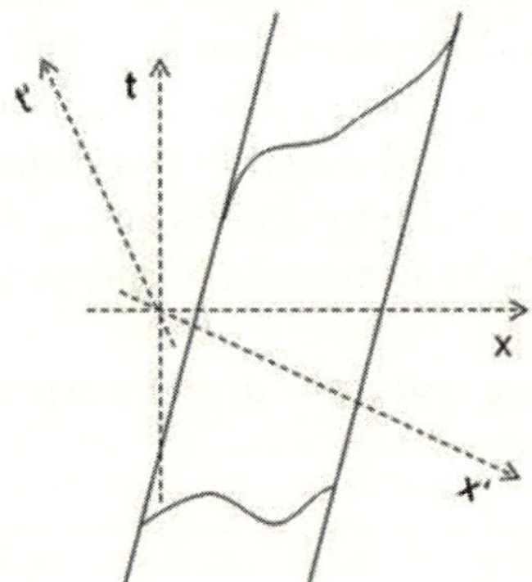

Fig. 3: A perduring whole with timelike and achronal but non-flat spatio-temporal parts. Does it exist and does it have color-properties also at those subregions?

As I would strongly suggest, this perduring object *never* exists at a timelike extended or at a curved spacelike region – namely at no (frame- or prime-) time.[29] And *a fortiori* it is neither red nor green, nor partly red and partly green at those regions.

Third point (concerning '*changing locations*' in spacetime): according to Balashov (2000b, 162) enduring objects "change their position in spacetime", while perduring objects are "atemporally confined to their locations in spacetime" (Balashov, 2005, 15). Enduring objects have "changing relations to other objects", while the perduring object has not – which leads, according to Balashov, to certain endurantist's commitments allegedly unwelcome for SR. Gibson and Pooley (see 2006, sec. 3.2) concede some grounds for the view that enduring objects change their locations in spacetime, although *they* are operating with the *timeless* block universe view, at least as I would read them. This shows, once again, that there is a strong intuition that endurantism is more 'dynamical' than perdurantism.

But: why so? Of course, Balashov and Gibson/Pooley do *not* think that enduring objects are moving through spacetime *in the way* that previously unoccupied spacelike-region are filled-up when time goes on. That would be McTaggart-contradictory (I guess), i.e., a contradiction of temporal predication which could only be avoided by introducing a (perhaps infinity of) meta-spacetime dimension(s). And it might in fact be conceivable that enduring objects change their locations in spacetime at least in some minimalist sense of the term, since an enduring object is directly *timelike separated* from itself (while a perduring object has temporal parts being timelike separated from each other): I will not argue with that. But why is this not also the case for the perduring object, in some other but equivalent way? The problem is that Balashov and Gibson/Pooley *agree* that enduring objects change their locations "with their proper time[s]" (Balashov, 2005, 14), while the perduring object does not so. But it is exactly the other way around: the *perduring* object changes its position with *its* proper-time; the enduring object has no proper-time at all but has proper-time-indexed properties or properties in a proper-time-indexed way.

Look at the following quotation from Gibson and Pooley:

> To the extent that one can make sense of an *enduring* object's proper time, this can be nothing other than the timelike distance along the spacetime curve composed of its locations. (Gibson/Pooley, 2006, 174; italics mine)

As you can see, Gibson and Pooley are somehow critical with respect to a 'too dynamical view' of the concept of proper-time. That is the reason why they concede Balashov *only some* grounds "but not enough to make Balashov's argument go through". I, once again, will not argue with that; my point is that Gibson and Pooley are spuriously talking about an *enduring* object. Only the *perduring* object, instead, could have a proper-time and one might then claim that:

To the extent that one can make sense of a *perduring* object's proper time, this can be nothing other than the timelike distance along the spacetime curve composed of its *temporal parts*.

Taking seriously the three eternalist readings of the sentence "a is F at t", namely a(t) is F (perdurantism), a is F(t) (indexicalism), and a is-t-ly F (adverbialism), one should not conceive of the perduring object as being something that is localized in spacetime *atemporally* – which would mean: *not* (proper-)time-indexed. And, correspondingly, one should not conceive of the enduring object as being something that is moving through spacetime by instantiating "incompatible properties at different moments of proper time" (Gibson/Pooley, 2006, 172) – which contradicts the view that their properties are proper-time-indexed (so, *compatible*) or being had in a proper-time-indexed way.

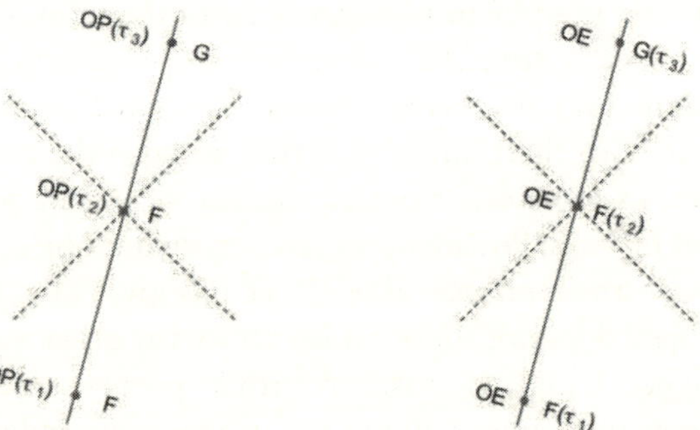

Fig. 4: The perduring object exists in spacetime by being proper-time-indexed, while the enduring object has its proper time only derivatively via its properties.

3. Conclusion

Assuming the *temporal* tenseless block universe view as the underlying eternalist hypothesis, it is unmotivated und unnatural to consider the perduring wholes as being singly located in spacetime, as having properties *simpliciter*, and as being "atemporally confined to their locations in spacetime" (Balashov, 2005, 15). And, independent from the specific block view, it is irrelevant to conceive of the perduring object this way in order to state the difference from endurantism: the perduring whole *is* multiply located in spacetime and only its temporal parts are singly located; the perduring whole has properties *only* relative to times (i. e., proper-times, frame-times etc.) and only its temporal parts have properties *simpliciter*; and, finally, a perduring whole *changes* its location in spacetime with *its* proper-time. The enduring object, in contrast, changes its location in spacetime by being (directly) timelike separated from itself, and by having time-indexed-properties or properties in a time-indexed way. Perdurantism is no less 'dynamical' than endurantism and, therefore, the "Asymmetry Thesis" is false.

Notes

1 Concerning this paper, it is sufficient to have in mind only *two* rivals, namely endurantism and traditional perdurantism. Exdurantism (see Haslanger, 2003), equivalent to Sider's stage view (see Sider, 2001, sec. 5.8), differs from perdurantism in the way that the 3-dimensional stages, in contrast to the 3-dimensional temporal parts of the worm, do not have only non-time-indexed properties *simpliciter* like "being red" but also certain temporally-loaded properties like "will be red". But this difference is irrelevant for my purposes.

2 Merricks (1995), however, has argued for endurantism being incompatible with eternalism (and perdurantism being incompatible with presentism), but meanwhile it is widely accepted that both views are compatible with eternalism (see, for many, Rea, 1998). According to the introduction of the endurance/perdurance distinction by Lewis (1986, 202 f.), both views rather *require* eternalism as the underlying hypothesis on temporal existence. I personally even agree on that view, although I don't think that presentism "rejects persistence altogether" (Lewis, 1986, 204), but that presentism needs a completely different theory of persistence and change.

3 Spatially extended objects, for example, in general do not have unique rest frames (see, however, Balashov, this volume).

4 "Dynamical" is in scare quotes, because a temporal dynamic such as characteristic for growing block or presentism is not intended.

5 A reformulation is needed, in *any* case regardless of spacetime being a relativistic one or not, for the following reason: classically, the B-theorist's primitive concept for an event is "being located at t", while for spacetime theories the primitive concept is rather "being located at p". In the former case the primitive implies (substantially) that a different event located at the same t is *simultaneous* with the given one, while a second event located at a different t' is *earlier or later* than the first. So, "being located at t" has already a temporal content. In the latter case, however, the primitive implies only the *triviality* (I would say) that a different event located at the

same p *coincides* with the given one, while a second event located at a different p' is *not* automatically earlier or later than the first (not even within Neo-Newtonian spacetime). So, "being located at p" has, without further specifications, no temporal content.

6 It is often said that there is a certain analogy between eternalism and modal realism: but note that modal realism is likewise *underdetermined* by the claim that all the possible is real, since it is *not* a matter of convenience but has an objective meaning what is *actual*. So, one could hold that it should not be a matter of convenience what exists *at t*.

7 See, however, Tooley, who, while defending his *dynamic* growing block view, characterizes the *static* view of temporal existence in exactly that way: "all temporal states of affairs are actual as of all times" (Tooley, 1997, 41).

8 From the fact that "the breaking down of spacetime into spaces at different times is not of fundamental import, but a matter of convenience" (Saunders, 2002, 281), Saunders concludes that SR is incompatible with *presentism*, while perfectly in accordance with eternalism, since: "that is precisely what the *tenseless* theory says". According to the NTT, however, it is indeed a matter of convenience which event is *present*, but it is *not* conventional what exists *at t*.

9 Note that *tensed* existence, at least for the presentists, is *not* a perspectival sense of "existence", since, according to them, there is no alternative to existing now. Thus for the presentists the *non*-perspectival sense of "existence" is tensed – Def (presentism): Tensed Existence [*simpliciter*]: event e exists *simpliciter* iff e presently exists (see, analogously, Hestevold/Carter, 2002, 499). Eternalism differs from presentism by the (substantial) claim that the non-perspectival sense of "existence" is temporally restrictable by a perspectival sense of "existence".

10 "Newton 2" *entails* a characterization of a moment of B-time within that spacetime, namely a hypersurface containing all and only events that exist in the same perspectival way.

11 In contrast, temporal succession in the presentist's sense must be independent of the earlier-later relation; the single 'ever changing present' implies a temporal difference that is more fundamental than the earlier-later relation between numerically different times.

12 While *not* differing in meaning.

13 A moment of B-time (a moment of cosmic time t_C) within those spacetimes is then a hypersurface on which all and only events exist in the same perspectival way.

14 Let aside the rhetorical use of „future" or "past", what Putnam substantially has in mind are events that are objectively (invariantly) earlier or later than a given p, which implies only B-theoretical descriptions.

15 So, the family of sentences for a given e – "p_nRe" – contains only sentences that are true (atemporally) or only sentences that are false (atemporally).

16 Although it contains, of course, events being "timelike" separated – but that is not enough for a concept of *temporal existence*.

17 In virtue of being an A-theory the world is conceived of being 'dynamical'

in a certain sense of the term, reflecting the idea of transitory presentness. But the world is in this case essentially, namely existentially, *static*.

18 It is not intended that Stein (1968) is a point eternalist, since according to him all events on and within the so-called 'past'-lightcone are realized with respect to p, as well. But this difference is irrelevant for my purposes, because including invariantly earlier events into the perspectival sense of "existence" does *not* lead to a growing block view which rather results by cutting the 'future' from the *non*-perspectival sense of "existence".

19 Note that Balashov is, in my interpretation, after an alternative to point eternalism: According to Putnam's view there would only be a coexistence relation in the general sense, which is out of interest for Balashov. According to point eternalism there would indeed be an interesting (restricted) coexistence relation but insufficiently strong, namely the way that each event coexists (in the interesting sense) *only with itself*.

20 From "Balashov 2" follows that the 'topological present' of a given p represents a moment of B-time, since all events located there exist in the same perspectival way. That is strange, however, because many of them are timelike separated from each other (see, analogously, Gilmore's reply, 2002, 246), so that Balashov has to argue for the view that each object, even a non-persisting event being located at some single point in spacetime, exists in *several* perspectival ways and in several others not, since it is located in the elsewhere of many different p but in the 'past'- or 'future'-lightcone of many others.

21 The challenge of SR for NTT is hence answered in the way that it might be in fact a matter of convenience what exists *at t*, since it remains invariant what exists in the non-perspectival way (which, perhaps, is not so for the presentist's view). But note that then the analogy of eternalism with modal realism breaks down, since, given a possible world, it is not a matter of convenience what is actual with respect to that world.

22 I want to suggest that one could also defend the corresponding claim: if we presuppose the *timeless* tenseless block universe view, endurantism is as 'static' as perdurantism.

23 Analogous to universal properties being multi-located in space, it is said, enduring objects are multi-located in time. This means in the framework of SR that an enduring object would be multi-located along a timelike curve if it is a spatially unextended object or on timelike separated spacelike regions if it is a spatially extended thing.

24 The relation between the perduring object and the spacetime region at which it is exactly located is intended to be one-one (as opposed to one-many), which, however, holds primarily for an instantaneous object (or event).

25 So, relativistically, it has either proper-time-indexed properties, frame-time-indexed properties, or spacelike-region-indexed properties.

26 These differences are well-known in the analytic philosophy of persistence. The indexicalist version is defended, for example, by van Inwagen (1990); a proponent for adverbialism is, for example, Haslanger (1989). For an application to spacetime physics see Balashov (2000a).

27 One might argue that an enduring object could have both time-indexed and non-time-indexed properties. A non-time-indexed property, however, is not a property that an object has *at all times*. It would rather be had *timelessly* which is in tension with the *temporal* tenseless block view.

28 Note that my view of perdurantism does *not* turn out to be exdurantism, since the temporal parts are conceived of as having *only* non-time-indexed properties *simpliciter*, while the stages have in addition to them also *temporally-loaded* properties like "will be red". For, according to counterpart theory, it is the given stage that has a (modal or) temporal property if its counterpart has the corresponding property *simpliciter*.

29 Note, once again, that the underlying eternalist hypothesis has, in our case, the specific sense of the *temporal* tenseless block view. Assuming, in contrast, the *timeless* view, for something "to exist at no time" does not imply that it *never* exists.

30 At this point Balashov considers spatially unextended objects. Spatially extended objects might not have any rest frame and hence no proper time would be available for them (but see Balashov, this volume). In those cases an adequate substitute (frame times or flat spacelike regions) is needed.

References

Balashov, Yuri, 2000a: Persistence and Spacetime: Philosophical Lessons of the Pole and Barn. In: *The Monist* 83, pp. 321–340.

Balashov, Yuri, 2000b: Enduring and Perduring Objects in Minkowski Spacetime. In: *Philosophical Studies* 99, pp. 129–166.

Balashov, Yuri, 2005: Special relativity, Coexistence and Temporal Parts: A Reply to Gilmore. In: *Philosophical Studies* 124, pp. 1–40.

Balashov, Yuri, 2008: Persistence and Multilocation in Spacetime. In: Dieks, Dennis (ed.): *The Ontology of Spacetime II*. Amsterdam: Elsevier, pp. 59–81.

Barker, Stephen; Dowe, Phil, 2003: Paradoxes of multi-location. In: *Analysis* 63.2, pp. 106–114.

Dorato, Mauro, 2006: Absolute Becoming, Relational Becoming, and the Arrow of Time. In: *Studies in History and Philosophy of Modern Physics*, 37.3, pp. 559–576.

Gibson, Ian; Pooley, Oliver, 2006: Relativistic Persistence. In: Hawthorne, John (ed.): *Philosophical Perspectives*, 20: *Metaphysics*. Blackwell: Malden, pp 157–198.

Gilmore, Cody, 2002: Balashov on Special Relativity, Coexistence, and Temporal Parts. In: *Philosophical Studies* 109, pp. 241–263.

Gilmore, Cody, 2006: Where in the relativistic world are we?. In: Hawthorne, John (ed.): *Philosophical Perspectives*, 20: *Metaphysics*. Malden: Blackwell, pp. 199–236.

Haslanger, Sally, 1989: Endurance and Temporary Intrinsics. In: *Analysis* 49:3, pp. 119–125.

Haslanger, Sally, 2003: Persistence Through Time. In: Loux, Michael L.; Zimmerman, Dean W. (eds.): *The Oxford Handbook of Metaphysics*, Oxford/New York: OUP, pp. 316–354.

Hestevold, Scott H.; Carter, William R., 2002: On Presentism, Endurance, and Change. In: *Canadian Journal of Philosophy* 32/4, pp. 491–510.

Inwagen, Peter van, 1990: Four-Dimensional Objects. In: *Nous* 24, pp. 245–255.

Lewis, David, 1986: *On the Plurality of Worlds*. Oxford/Malden: Blackwell.

Mellor, Hugh D., 1981: *Real Time*. Cambridge: CUP.

Merricks, Trenton, 1995: On the Incompatibility of Enduring and Perduring Entities. In: *Mind* 104, pp. 523–531.

Putnam, Hilary, 1967: Time and Physical Geometry. In: *The Journal of Philosophy* 64, pp. 240–247.

Rea, Michael C., 1998: Temporal Parts Unmotivated. In: *The Philosophical Review* 107, pp. 225–260.

Saunders, Simon, 2002: How Relativity Contradicts Presentism. In: Callender, Craig (ed.): *Time, Reality, and Experience*. Cambridge: CUP, pp. 277–292.

Sider, Theodore, 2001: *Four-Dimensionalism. An Ontology of Persistence and Time*. Oxford: Clarendon Press.

Stein, Howard, 1968: On Einstein-Minkowski Space-Time. In: *The Journal of Philosophy*, 65, pp. 5–23.

Tooley, Michael, 1997: *Time, Tense, and Causation*. Oxford: Clarendon Press.

Cody Gilmore

Keep in touch

Abstract

I introduce a puzzle about contact and de re temporal predication in relativistic spacetime. In particular, I describe an apparent counterexample to the following principle, roughly stated: if B is never in a position to say 'I was touching A, I am touching A, and I will be touching A', then (time travel aside) A is never in a position to say 'I was touching B, I am touching B, and I will be touching B'. In the case I present, the most that A is ever in a position to say is: 'I am now touching B, but this is the only instant at which this will ever be so'. B, on the other hand, can say: 'I was formerly touching A, I am currently touching A, and I will in the future be touching A'. (And neither object is a time traveler.)

Zusammenfassung

Ich präsentiere ein Rätsel über Kontakt und temporale *de re* Prädikation in relativistischer Raumzeit. Genauer gesagt, beschreibe ich ein augenscheinliches Gegenbeispiel zu folgendem Prinzip: Wenn B niemals berechtigterweise sagen kann, „Ich habe A berührt, berühre gerade A und werde A berühren", so ist (Zeitreisen außer Betracht gelassen) auch A niemals gerechtfertigt zu sagen, „Ich habe B berührt, berühre gerade B und werde B berühren". In dem dargestellten Fall aber ist A höchstens einmal in der Lage zu sagen: „Ich berühre jetzt gerade B, aber das ist der einzige Augenblick, in dem dies jemals der Fall sein wird". B dagegen kann sagen: „Ich habe A zuvor berührt, berühre A gegenwärtig und werde A auch in Zukunft berühren". (Und keiner von beiden ist ein Zeitreisender.)

Introduction

This paper introduces a puzzle about contact and de re temporal predication in relativistic spacetime. I consider a series of responses to the puzzle without endorsing any of them. The discussion is set within a stage theoretic[1] framework, not because I think that the puzzle poses a special problem for stage theory, but merely because the view is associated with a relatively explicit account of de re temporal predication. I strongly suspect that worm theory and endurantism confront more or less the same puzzle and have a parallel range of responses available to them, with similar costs and benefits, though I won't try to argue for that here.

1. A Story

You, A, are a *Line* – a continuous, straight, spatially one-dimensional material object of finite length. Your beloved, B, is a *Point* – a spatially zero-dimensional material point particle. Your only desire is for some lasting contact with others (preferably your beloved). More specifically, you want to be able to say, 'I *was* touching someone, I *am* touching someone, and I *will be* touching someone.'[2] You want that sentence, as uttered by you at some moment of your life, to be true. More or less equivalently, you want there to be a time in your life when you are in a position to think (correctly) that you were formerly touching someone, that you are currently touching someone, and that you will in the future be touching someone. You ask the oracle whether you will ever get your wish. It answers thus:

> You and your beloved will one day move toward one another on a pathway. You will approach, touch, and recede. But this episode will be very brief. Indeed, you make contact at only a single spacetime point. And since the two of you are mutually impenetrable, you do not spatiotemporally overlap: no point belongs both to your spacetime path and to your beloved's spacetime path. Here is a spacetime diagram of your encounter. (See Figure 1.)
>
> Each of you will live forever, but only on this occasion will the two of you be in contact, and you will never be in contact with anyone else. (And no one travels backward in time or traces out a closed timelike curve, etc.) The oracle has spoken.

Your sister, who has accompanied you on your visit to the oracle, offers consoling words. 'Ah well ... you win some and you lose some ... there's more to life than lasting contact ... and anyway, an instant of contact is better than none at all ...,' and so on. But you've never been happier. 'Don't you see?,' you say. 'I'm going to get the only thing I've ever wanted!'

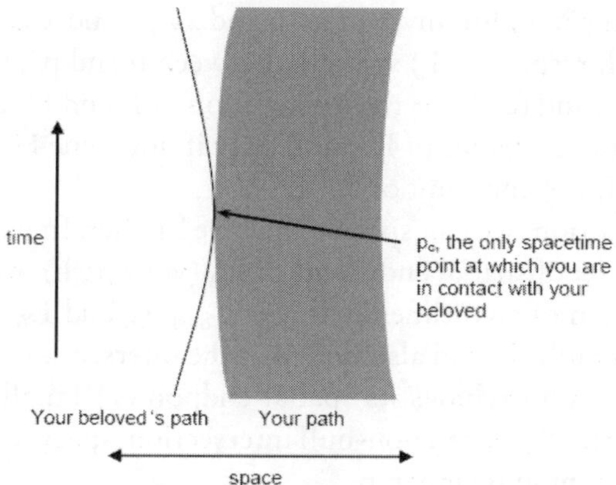

Figure 1

2. The Argument for Optimism

2.1 A More Precise Description of the Case

You and your beloved inhabit Minkowski spacetime. Your beloved exists at all times and is spatially point-like throughout his career. His spacetime path,[3] R_B, is a timelike line.[4]

You, A, also exist at all times and are, throughout your career, spatially linelike and topologically open at both ends. To be more precise, let R_A be your path or 'worldsheet'. Then for any inertial reference frame F and for any hyperplane[5] H associated with F, there are distinct points p_{H1} and p_{H2} such that the intersection of H and R_A is the set whose members are those points in H that are (with respect to F) spatially between p_{H1} and p_{H2}, where this set excludes those two points themselves. Informally, the idea is that your 'spatial locations' are line segments that do not include their endpoints.

To describe the encounter in a bit more detail, it will help to have some definitions in hand. First I want to make precise the notion of a *spatial endpoint* of the relevant sort of worldsheet, where a worldsheet may or may not include its spatial endpoints. (Yours doesn't.) I will say that p is a *spatial <H, F>-endpoint* of R if and only if: (i) F is an inertial reference frame, (ii) H is a hyperplane associated with F, (iii) p belongs to H, and (iv) there is a region R_H and a point p* such that: (a) p* belongs to H, (b) R_H includes every point in H that is (with respect to F) spatially between p and p*, (c) for any x, if $x \neq p$ and $x \neq p^*$ and x is not a point in H that is (with respect to F) spatially between p and p*, then x is not a member of R_H, and (d) R_H = the intersection of R and H. I will then say that p is a *spatial endpoint* of R if and only if: for some H and some F, p is a spatial <H, F>-endpoint of R.

Using this notion, we can specify the case further. In particular, if we let R_{EA} be the set of spatial endpoints of R_A (your path), we can add that R_{EA} is the union of two timelike lines, $L_{YourLeftE}$ and $L_{YourRightE}$, whose intersection is null. We can also note that the intersection of R_A and R_{EA} is null. (Your path excludes its spatial endpoints.) Finally, we can say that $L_{YourLeftE}$ and R_B have a non-null intersection: specifically, they have exactly one common member, p_c.

Now for four more definitions, which will help us pinpoint the sense in which you and your beloved *touch*.[6] First, say that R is an *open <H, F>-sphere* about p if and only if: (i) F is an inertial reference frame, (ii) H is a hyperplane associated with F, (iii) p is a point in H, and (iv) there is some spatial distance d such that R = {x: $x \in H$ & with respect to F, the distance from x to p is less than d}, that is, R is the set of those points in H whose distance from p with respect to F is less than d. Second, say that p is an *<H, F>-boundary point* of R if and only if: (i) F is an inertial reference frame, (ii) H is a hyperplane associated with F, (iii) each open <H, F>-sphere about p has a non-null intersection both with R and with H – R.[7] Third, say that p is a *regional contact point* between R_1 and R_2 if and only if: (i) R_1 and R_2 are regions whose intersection is null, (ii) for some H and some F, p is an <H, F>-boundary point of R_1, (iii) for some H and some F, p is an <H, F>-boundary point of R_2, and (iv) p belongs either to R_1 or to R_2. Fourth, say that o_1 *is touching* o_2 if and only if there is an R_1, an R_2, and a p such that: (i) p is a regional contact point between R_1 and R_2, (ii) o_1 exactly occupies R_1 and (iii) o_2 exactly occupies R_2.

Now, given these definitions together with our previous claims about the case, I take it that p_c is the one and only regional contact point between R_A (your path) and R_B (your beloved's path), and that p_c belongs to R_B, not R_A.

2.2 *An Optimistic Interpretation of the Case*

On the basis of these facts, you reason as follows. Let a *slice*[8] of a region be a non-null intersection between that region and some hyperplane.

Then there is a set S_A of slices of R_A that has the following property:

(i) it has continuum-many members,

(ii) each of its members is in regional contact with R_B at p_c,

(iii) there is *strict total order* R_{Pr} on S_A,[9] where R_{Pr} is set of ordered pairs of members of S_A such that $\langle R_1, R_2\rangle \in R_{Pr}$ iff:

(a) for each point p_1 in R_1, there is a point p_2 in R_2 such that p_1 is in the chronological past[10] of p_2,

(b) for each point p_2 in R_2, there is a point p_1 in R_1 such that p_1 is in the chronological past of p_2,

(c) no point in R_2 is identical to or in the causal past of any point in R_1.

We can think of R_{Pr} as corresponding to a relation of *being absolutely earlier than* that can hold between spatially extended spacelike regions in relativistic spacetimes.[11] In case one doubts the existence of such a set, consider the following diagram:

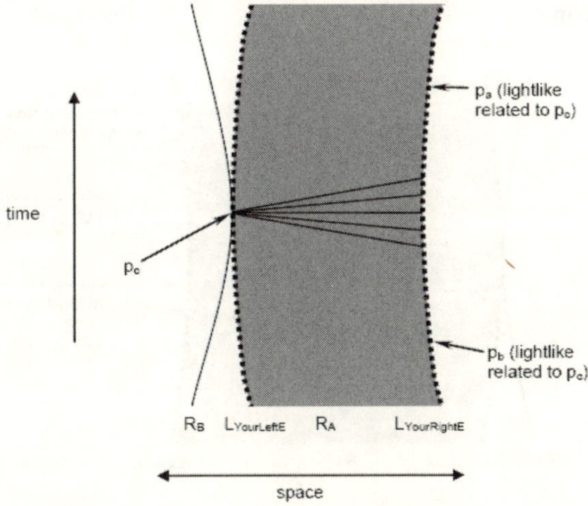

Figure 2

Put something in the set if and only if: (i) it is a line segment whose left endpoint is p_c and whose right endpoint lies on $L_{YourRightE}$ below p_a and above p_b (each of which is lightlike related to p_c), and (ii) it excludes both of its endpoints. (Notice that no two of these segments intersect. They all have the same left endpoint, but they all exclude that point, and they obviously don't intersect anywhere else.) It should be easy to convince oneself that this set corresponds in a straightforward way to a set of slices of R_A having the relevant features.

Now suppose that stage theory is true. (See note 1.) Ordinary objects such as you and your beloved are instantaneous stages. Such objects persist by having temporal counterparts (themselves instantaneous stages) existing at other times. Moreover, truth conditions for most de re temporal predications are given counterpart-theoretically. For example:

– the sentence type 'I *was* happy' is true as uttered by a stage s if and only if a past counterpart of s $is_{tenseless}$ happy,
– the sentence type 'I *am* happy' is true as uttered by a stage s if and only if s $is_{tenseless}$ happy, and
– the sentence type 'I *will be* happy' is true as uttered by a stage s if and only if a future counterpart of s $is_{tenseless}$ happy.

Given all this, it seems that you will get your wish. For it seems that there is a stage (e.g., Stage 2 in the diagram below) that is in a position to say, 'I was touching someone, I am touching someone, and I will be touching someone'.

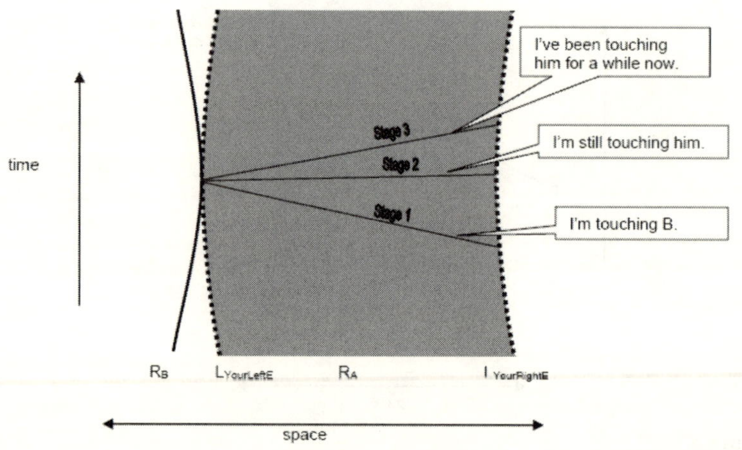

Figure 3

After all, Stage 1, Stage 2, and Stage 3 are all touching someone (namely, B), and Stage 1 and Stage 3 would seem to be past and future counterparts, respectively, of Stage 2.[12]

Suppose that you are Stage 2. Why think that Stage 3 is one of your future counterparts? The main reason can be broken down into four claims. First, Stage 3 is an instantaneous temporal part[13] of the 'you-worm' – the sum of you and all your temporal counterparts. For future reference, call it *Worm A*. (Your path is the region that it exactly occupies.) Second, Stage 3 resembles you very closely. In particular, Stage 3 is the same kind of thing you are and it is not missing any spatial parts of you.[14] Third, Stage 3 lies 'wholly in your future' in the sense that the region that you exactly occupy bears the *being absolutely earlier than* relation (described above) to the region that Stage 3 exactly occupies.[15] Stage 3 does not spatiotemporally overlap you, no part of it is even in the causal (not to mention chronological) past of any part of you, every part of it is in the chronological future of some part of you, and every part of you is in the chronological past of some part of it. Fourth, and relatedly, you stand in the appropriate immanent causal relation to Stage 3: Stage 3 is the way it is in large part because you are the way you are.[16]

In light of these facts, it is highly plausible that Stage 3 is one of your future counterparts. To reinforce this verdict, consider a fanciful thought-experiment. Continue to suppose that you are Stage 2. But now suppose, further, that Stage 3 is in extreme pain, and that it is the *only* temporal part of Worm A that is in pain of any kind.[17] What sort of attitude should you have toward this painful experience? The natural thing to say, it seems to me, is that it's appropriate for you to dread this pain. This suggests that Stage 3 is one of your future counterparts, since their pains are the only ones that it is appropriate for you to dread. (Analogous considerations support the verdict that Stage 1 is one of your past counterparts. I assume that these do not require separate discussion.)

Admittedly, Stages 1, 2, and 3 are associated with different inertial reference frames. But why should that matter? That fact by itself doesn't show that none of the given stages is a temporal counterpart of any of the others. Suppose that Obama is currently at rest with respect to the Oval Office, and call his current stage *O-stage-1*. All of O-stage-1's parts are simultaneous with respect to the inertial frame F_{ov} – the 'Oval Office frame'. Now suppose that later today, while flying aboard Air Force One, he will be at rest with respect to a *different* inertial frame, say, the frame F_{af1}. Pick one of those later stages and call it *O-stage-2*. All of its parts are simultaneous with respect to F_{af1}, but not with respect to F_{ov}. I take it to be just obvious that O-stage-2 is a temporal counterpart of O-stage-1 (and that any experiences that happen to O-stage-2 are ones that O-stage-1 is in position to anticipate). And yet those stages are associated with different inertial frames.

Of course, the two cases are different. O-stage-1 and O-stage 2 are both what we might think of, rather loosely, as 'rest frame stages' of Obama, whereas Stages 1 and 3 are not 'rest frame stages' of A. But the crucial point here is just this: the mere fact that Stages 1, 2, and 3 are associated with different inertial frames does not *by itself* guarantee that they are not temporal counterparts. We will return to these issues in section 3. (Eventually I will argue, among other things, that we should not limit a thing's temporal counterparts to its 'rest frame stages'.)

To recap, then, the situation is this. You are Stage 2, and you are, in the tenseless sense defined earlier, touching someone (namely B). This, I submit, is sufficient for the result that:

(1) 'I am touching someone' is true as uttered by Stage 2.

Moreover, Stage 1 is your past counterpart and is also touching B in the tenseless sense. This suffices for

(2) 'I was touching someone' is true as uttered by Stage 2.[18]

Finally, Stage 3 is your future counterpart and is touching B in that same sense. This yields

(3) 'I will be touching someone' is true as uttered by Stage 2.

I take it that if sentences S_1, S_2, and S_3 are each true as uttered by stage x, then the sentence $\ulcorner S_1, S_2$, and $S_3 \urcorner$ is also true as uttered by stage x. This gives us

(4) 'I was touching someone, I am touching someone, and I will be touching someone' is true as uttered by Stage 2.

So you get your wish.

One small point before we move on. For simplicity, I've set up the case in such a way that the stages in question exactly occupy flat regions associated with different inertial frames. But that's in no way essential to the puzzle. At the cost of some additional complexity (e.g., in our definitions of 'contact' and 'touching'), we could focus instead on a different case in which the stages exactly occupied a series of non-flat (but still spacelike) regions, none of which has any special connection to any particular inertial frame.[19] (See the diagram below.)

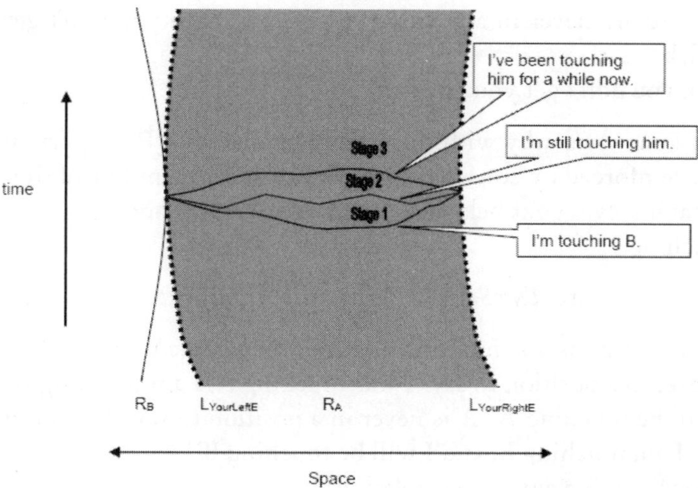

Figure 4

3. Pessimism

3.1 Motivating Pessimism

Isn't it obvious that something has gone wrong here? For there seems to be a compelling argument for an opposing conclusion:

The First Pessimistic Argument

P1 If a persisting point-particle makes contact with a persisting line-segment at just a single spacetime point, if nothing else ever makes contact with the persisting line-segment, and if nothing travels backward in time (etc.),[20] then the persisting line segment is never in a position to say (correctly), 'I was touching someone, I am touching someone, and I will be touching someone'.

P2 You are a persisting line segment, a persisting point-particle makes contact with you at just a single spacetime point, nothing else ever makes contact with you, and nothing travels backward in time (etc.).

C1 So, you are never in a position to say (correctly), 'I was touching someone, I am touching someone, and I will be touching someone'.

P3 If you are never in a position to say that, then you don't get your wish.

C2 So, you don't get your wish.

I have some sympathy with this argument and with P1 in particular. It can be reinforced by considering a somewhat different line of thought – one that involves your beloved's perspective and the apparent symmetry of touching:

The Second Pessimistic Argument

P4 If touching is a symmetric relation, then (time travel aside) if B is never in a position to say 'I was touching A, I am touching A, and I will be touching A', A is never in a position to say, 'I was touching B, I am touching B, and I will be touching B'.

P5 Touching is a symmetric relation.

P6 B is never in a position to say 'I was touching A, I am touching A, and I will be touching A'.

C3 So, A is never in a position to say 'I was touching B, I am touching B, and I will be touching B'.

P7 If A is never in a position to say 'I was touching B, I am touching B, and I will be touching B', and if A never touches anyone other than B, then A is never in a position to say 'I was touching someone, I am touching someone, and I will be touching someone'.

P8 A never touches anyone other than B.

C4 So, A is never in a position to say 'I was touching someone, I am touching someone, and I will be touching someone'.

This leads, as before, to the conclusion that you don't get your wish. One key premise in this argument, and the only one that I take to require comment, is P6. To see why it's plausible, note that there is only one 'B-stage' that touches Worm A or any 'A-stage'. The B-stage in question is the one that exactly occupies the region, call it R_c, whose sole member is p_c. Call the given stage *Stage 4*. Stage 4 is in a position to say 'I am touching A', but no other B-stage is in a position to say that. And since no past or future counterpart of Stage 4 touches any part of Worm A, Stage 4 is not in a position to say 'I was touching A' or 'I will be touching A'. So no B-stage whatever is in a position to say 'I was touching A, I am touching A, and I will be touching A'. In other words, B is never in a position to utter the given sentence.

This leaves us with a puzzle. We have an apparently convincing case for the conclusion that you do get your wish and a perhaps equally convincing case for the conclusion that you don't get your wish.

3.2 Some Objections to the Case for Optimism

Objection One: Relativize to inertial frames. The Case for Optimism saddles the stage theorist with the assumption that he must provide an account of the notion of a *sentence type's being true as uttered by a stage.* This is a *dyadic* notion of truth, with a slot for a sentence type and a slot for a stage. But the stage theorist is under no burden to accept this assumption. An alternative and perhaps more appropriate target is a notion of truth that is at least triadic, with a slot for a sentence type, a slot for a (presumably *inertial*) reference frame, a slot for an instant of time in (or hyperplane associated with) that frame, and perhaps additional slots – e.g., for the speaker. Here is how Sider puts it:

> The stage theorist should provide an account of a somewhat theoretical notion, that of *a sentence type's being true as uttered at a time t, understood relative to frame of reference F.* The stage theorist should claim, for example, that the sentence type 'Ted will be bald', as uttered at t, interpreted relative to F, is true iff the Ted-stage at t, relative to F, has a temporal counterpart in the future, relative to F, that is bald. (Sider 2001, 199).

How does this help? Put very crudely, the idea is this. Relative to any inertial frame F, there is only a single instant at which A is touching B (or anyone). So, relative to any inertial frame F and instant t in F, the sentence 'I was touching someone, I am touching someone, and I will be touching someone', as uttered by the A-stage corresponding to <t, F>, is not true.

To spell this out fully, recall that A's wish is to be in a position to say 'I was touching someone, I am touching someone, and I will be touching someone'. Now, if

(i) the only notion of truth for sentence types that can be made sense of in a relativistic context is the one Sider focuses on,

then presumably

(ii) A's wish is satisfied if and only if there is an inertial frame F and an instant t in F such that the relevant sentence is *true as uttered (by some A-stage) at t understood relative to F.*

Moreover, it's clear that

(iii) there is no such <instant t, inertial frame F> pair.

For

(iv) the sentence type 'I was touching someone, I am touching someone, and I will be touching someone' is true as uttered by an A-stage x at an instant t relative to an inertial frame F if and only if there are hyperplanes H_P, H_t, and H_F of 'simultaneity-with-respect-to-F' such that:
   (a) H_t is the hyperplane corresponding to <t, F>,
   (b) H_P is earlier-with-respect-to-F than H_t,
   (c) H_F is later-with-respect-to-F than H_t,
   (d) x is the A-stage that exactly occupies the intersection of R_A and H_t and x is touching someone,
   (e) x has a (past) temporal counterpart that exactly occupies the intersection of R_A and H_P and that is touching someone, and
   (f) x has a (future) temporal counterpart that exactly occupies the intersection of R_A and H_F and that is touching someone.

In short, the given sentence is true as uttered by an A-stage x at t with respect to inertial frame F if and only if x is the <t, F>-slice of Worm A, x is touching someone, and x has, as temporal counterparts, earlier and later 'F-slices' of the A-worm that are themselves touching someone.

And the right-hand side of the biconditional in (iv) is false. Pick any inertial frame F. There will be exactly one instant t associated with F such that the <t, F>-slice of the A-worm is touching someone. Hence, for any inertial frame F and instant t in F, if the <t, F> slice of the A-worm is touching someone, then that slice does *not* have, as temporal counterparts, earlier or later F-slices of the A-worm that are themselves touching someone. (See Figure 5.)

There is no <t, F> pair with respect to which the given sentence is true. And since the only sense in which the given sentence could be true is relative to some <t, F> pair, there is no sense in which the sentence is true.

Reply. Ian Gibson and Oliver Pooley (2006: 160–163) have argued that there is a tendency in the literature on persistence and relativity to rely too heavily on the notion of an *inertial reference frame* and the associated notion of a *hyperplane* – i.e., a maximal spacelike hypersurface that

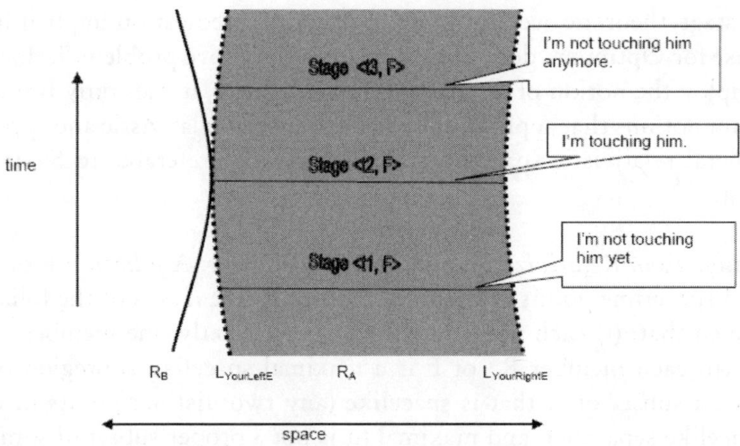

Figure 5

is *flat*. In connection with Sider's definition of the notion of an instantaneous temporal part (a definition that makes heavy use of the notion of an inertial reference frame), they write:

> While flat regions of spacetime are in some sense geometrically privileged, there is no reason to suppose that this gives them any special metaphysical status, in the context of questions about persistence or otherwise. More significantly, one surely wants a definition applicable the context of our best theory of space and time, general relativity. While this theory allows spacetimes containing flat spacelike regions, generic matter-filled worldtubes will have no flat maximal spacelike subregions (2006: 163).

I agree[21] and would only add that one also surely wants an *account of the truth conditions of de re temporal predications* applicable in general relativity. Inertial frames are not, in general,[22] available there.

Let me be explicit about the problem this causes for Sider's account, if that account were applied in a general relativistic spacetime that contains no inertial frames. (In fairness to Sider, his account is intended for Minkowski spacetime only.) Suppose that we inhabit such a spacetime, and consider the sentence 'I was a boy'. Sider's account delivers the result that this sentence is not true as uttered by me now (by my present stage), since there is no inertial frame F such that I have, as a temporal counterpart, an F-slice of the Cody-worm that is: (i) earlier-with-respect-to-F than my present stage and (ii) a boy. But that sentence is true as uttered by me now. So Sider's account is incorrect.

The stage-theoretic account of de re temporal predication implicit in the Case for Optimism does not suffer from the above problem. It does not employ the notion of an inertial frame. Instead, it uses only frame invariant notions that apply equally in both special relativistic and typical general relativistic spacetimes. This makes it preferable to Sider's account.

Objection Two: Relativize to foliations of spacetime. A *foliation* F of a set R of spacetime points is a set of *subsets* of R (the *leaves* of the foliation) such that: (i) each point in R belongs to exactly one member of F and (ii) each member R* of F is a maximal spacelike subregion of R – i.e., a subset of R that is spacelike (any two distinct points in it are spacelike separated) and maximal (it is not a proper subset of some other spacelike subset of R). Informally, a foliation of a region is a way of exhaustively slicing that region into a series of non-intersecting, temporally unextended (but not necessarily flat) *leaves.*

Typical general relativistic spacetimes do not contain inertial reference frames but do admit of foliations. This suggests an emended version of Sider's account that offers truth conditions in terms of the notion of *a sentence type's being true as uttered at a leaf l in a foliation f of spacetime.* Specifically, the emended account says that

(iv*) the sentence type 'I was touching someone, I am touching someone, and I will be touching someone' is true as uttered by an A-stage x at a leaf l in a foliation f of spacetime if and only if there are leaves l_P and l_F of f such that:
- (a) l_P is earlier-with-respect-to-f than l
- (b) l_F is later-with-respect-to-f than l
- (c) x is the A-stage that exactly occupies the intersection of R_A and l, and x is touching[23] someone
- (d) x has a (past) temporal counterpart that exactly occupies the intersection of R_A and l_P and that is touching someone, and
- (e) x has a (future) temporal counterpart that exactly occupies the intersection of R_A and l_F and that is touching someone.

In short, the given sentence is true as uttered by a given A-stage x at an f-leaf l if and only if x is the l-slice of Worm A, x is touching someone, and x has, as temporal counterparts, earlier and later 'f-slices' of Worm A that are themselves touching someone. (An f-slice of a worm is a temporal part of that worm that exactly occupies the intersection of the worm's path and some leaf in the foliation f.)

As with (iv), the right-hand side of the biconditional in (iv*) is false. Pick any foliation f of spacetime as a whole. Exactly one leaf, l_c, of f, will intersect B's path, R_B, at the 'contact point' p_c. This leaf will also intersect A's path, R_A, at a certain region, $R_A \cap l_c$. The temporal part of Worm A that exactly occupies $R_A \cap l_c$ will touch (in a suitably generalized sense) Worm B at the contact point. But, I assume, no other 'f-slice' of Worm A will touch Worm B.

(Intuitively, such an f-slice – call it *slice** – would need to have parts that are spacelike separated from p_c and 'arbitrarily spatially close' to p_c. Now, since slice* would belong to a different leaf, l*, in the original foliation (f), l* would need to intersect R_B at some point p* that is timelike separated from p_c. But if slice* contains parts that are spacelike separated from p_c and arbitrarily spatially close to it, and if p_c is timelike separated from p*, then presumably some of slice*'s parts are also timelike separated from p*. And slice*'s parts, along with p*, are all supposed to be associated with the same leaf, l*. This gives us the result that l* contains timelike related entities, contrary to our assumption that l* is a leaf in a foliation and hence spacelike.)

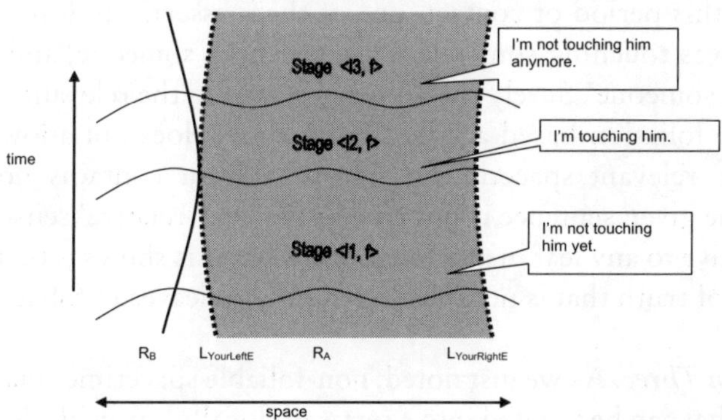

Figure 6

If all of this is correct, then there is no leaf in any foliation of spacetime with respect to which the given sentence (as uttered by some A-stage) is true.

Reply. There are general relativistic spacetimes (e.g., the Gödel spacetime) that do not admit of global foliations.[24] Presumably our account of the truth conditions of de re temporal predications ought not entail that the given sentence can never be uttered truly in such spacetimes, regardless of what goes on in them. But the account sketched above entails just that.

Let me elaborate. There are large, four-dimensional 'chunks' of the Gödel spacetime that are intrinsically very similar to chunks of 'ordinary' foliable spacetimes that lack closed timelike curves (CTCs).[25] These chunks, even when embedded in the Gödel spacetime, admit of 'local' foliations – foliations into 'locally' spacelike leaves.[26]

Now, to see why this is relevant, suppose that the Gödel spacetime contains language users much like ourselves but that they (and indeed all living things in the Gödel spacetime) are confined to a four-dimensional chunk that is intrinsically very similar to some chunk from an ordinary foliable spacetime devoid of CTCs. Suppose that the life-containing chunk is spatially very large – say, the size of a supercluster of galaxies – and temporally quite long – say, 7 billion years long. Further, suppose that the living things in it are confined to a single planet and to a time span of just one billion years. Suppose that the language-users speak English (or something qualitatively just like it), and that two of them come into perfect contact for several hours (locally speaking). Midway through this period of contact, one of them assertively utters the sentence 'I was touching someone, I am touching someone, and I will be touching someone'. Surely the sentence is true in the relevant context.

But the foliation-based account given above does not allow for this. Since the relevant spacetime is non-foliable, it contains no 'leaves'. Hence the given sentence is not true in the 'leaf-relative' sense: it is not true relative to any leaf in any foliation. What this shows is that we need a notion of truth that is not relativized only to leaves in foliations.

Objection Three. As we just noted, non-foliable spacetimes may contain regions that can be foliated into a series of 'locally' spacelike leaves. Presumably the path of any ordinary persisting object can be so foliated. We might then offer a second emendation of Sider's account in terms of the notion of *a sentence type's being true as uttered at a leaf l in 'local foliation' f*, where f need not be a foliation of spacetime as whole. This emended account might be expected to yield the following analogue of (iv) and (iv*):

(iv**) the sentence type 'I was touching someone, I am touching someone, and I will be touching someone' is true as uttered by an A-stage x at a leaf l in a local foliation f of a region R if and only if there are leaves l_P and l_F of f such that:
(a) l_P is earlier-with-respect-to-f than l,
(b) l_F is later-with-respect-to-f than l,
(c) x is the A-stage that exactly occupies the intersection of R_A and l, and x is touching[27] someone,
(d) x has a (past) temporal counterpart that exactly occupies the intersection of R_A and l_P and that is touching someone, and
(e) x has a (future) temporal counterpart that exactly occupies the intersection of R_A and l_F and that is touching someone.

Unlike (iv) or (iv*), this account allows that the given sentence can be uttered truly even in nonfoliable spacetimes.

Reply. Yes, but (iv**) also differs from its predecessors in another way: it fails to block the Case for Optimism. For there are leaves in local foliations with respect to which the given sentence, as uttered by an A-stage, is true. In particular, A's path, R_A, *can* be foliated into (non-intersecting) locally spacelike slices many of which are in contact with R_B at p_c. A glance at Figure 7 should make this clear.

Call the relevant foliation f*. Now pick the 'horizontal' leaf l_2 that is in contact with R_c at p_c. This leaf is exactly occupied by an entity, call it *Stage 2*, that is a temporal part of Worm A and an 'A-stage'. Now consider the not-quite-horizontal lines that are, respectively, directly above and below the line corresponding to leaf l_h. These lines correspond, respectively, to leaves l_3 and l_1, each of which is also in contact with R_c at p_c. Leaf l_1 is exactly occupied by Stage 1, and l_3 is exactly occupied by Stage 3, where each of these stages is also: (i) a temporal part of Worm A, (ii) a temporal counterpart of Stage 2, and (iii) touching a certain B-stage, hence touching someone. According to (iv**), then, the given sentence is *true* as uttered by Stage 2 at leaf l_2 in the local foliation f*. So once again, you get your wish.

Objection Four. Ordinary objects are stages. The sum of an ordinary object and all of its temporal counterparts is an 'o-worm'. Time travel cases aside, all ordinary objects and temporal counterparts thereof are instantaneous temporal parts of o-worms. More specifically, for any ordinary object o1 and any temporal counterpart o2 of o1, o1 and o2 are

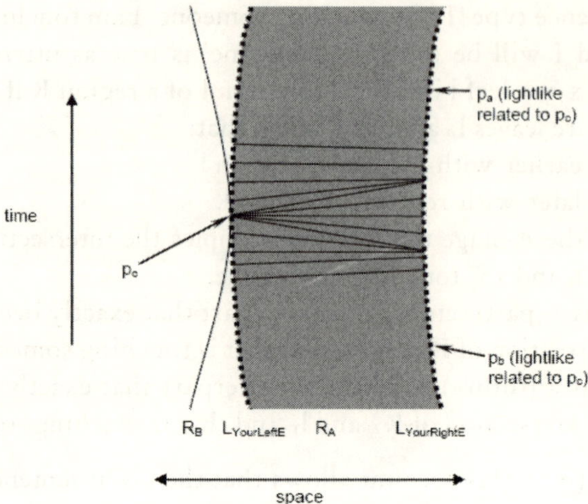

Figure 7

each instantaneous temporal parts of the 'o1-worm' – the sum of o1 and all of o1's temporal counterparts.

But not all instantaneous temporal parts of o-worms are ordinary objects or temporal counterparts thereof. We already knew this on the basis of the 'corner slice' example from Gilmore (2006, 212). (See note 13 for further discussion.) But now we can see that an even more extreme position is required. Indeed, it turns out that *relatively few* instantaneous temporal parts of an o-worm are ordinary objects or temporal counterparts thereof. In particular:

RF For any x, any y, and any z, if x is an ordinary object, if y is a temporal counterpart of x, and if z is the sum of x and all of x's temporal counterparts, then there is a region R and a set f such that:
- (i) R is the region that z exactly occupies,
- (ii) f is a local foliation of R,
- (iii) f is the 'z rest frame foliation' of R: i. e., of all the local foliations of R, f is the one that, roughly put, does the best job of slicing R into leaves whose points are simultaneous-with-respect-to-z's rest frame at the relevant moment of z's career,
- (iv) x exactly occupies some leaf in f, and
- (v) y exactly occupies some leaf in f.

According to RF, an entity is an ordinary object or a temporal counterpart of one only if that entity is a 'rest-frame-slice' of the corresponding worm.[28] Admittedly, there are serious doubts as to whether the notion of a rest-frame-foliation of a region can be made sense of.[29] But suppose for the sake of argument that it can. Presumably Worm A has only one rest-frame-slice that touches Worm B,[30] in which case, given RF together with plausible assumptions about the truth conditions of the sentence in question, there is no A-stage with respect to which that sentence is true. And in that case, you don't get your wish.

Reply. Concerns about the notion of a 'rest frame foliation' aside, the above strategy succeeds in blocking the Case for Optimism. But it faces a very serious problem of its own – essentially just stage-theoretic version of the problem for endurantism described in Gilmore (2006, 220–222) and (2008). I am an ordinary object, and so is each of my red blood cells. Pick one of them, and call it *BC*. BC is currently in motion relative to me. I've been sedentary throughout the last second or two and I will continue to be sedentary for the next few seconds. BC, meanwhile, has been moving rapidly upward, from my left foot toward my heart, and will continue to do so for the next few seconds. As a result, the relevant section of BC's path (the one stretching from 2 seconds ago to two seconds from now) is not parallel to the relevant section of my path. Accordingly, the rest-frame-slices of BC's path (in the relevant section) are not subregions of the rest-frame-slices of my path. But, given RF, this entails, absurdly, that the sentence 'BC is a part of Cody' is not true as uttered by me now.

To see why, note first that given stage theory and RF, the name 'BC' will refer to some rest-frame-slice S_{BC} of the BC-worm, where this slice is confined to the section of that worm in question. Likewise, the name 'Cody' will refer to some rest-frame-slice S_{Cody} of the Cody-worm, where this slice is also confined to the section of *that* worm in question. Now let R_{BC} be the region that S_{BC} exactly occupies, and let R_{Cody} be the region that S_{Cody} exactly occupies. Since the relevant slices are *rest*-frame-slices of the relevant paths, and since the relevant paths fail to be parallel throughout the relevant period, we get the result that R_{BC} fails to be a subregion of R_{Cody}. (To be sure, R_{BC} is a subregion of the region occupied by the Cody-worm, and R_{BC} intersects a great many rest-frame-slices of that region, but it isn't a subregion of any of them.) But for any x and any y, if the region that x exactly occupies is not a subregion of the region that y exactly occupies, then x is not a part of y.[31] So S_{BC} is not a part of S_{Cody}. So the referent of 'BC', as uttered by me now, is not a part (*simpliciter* and in the tenseless sense) of the referent of 'Cody', as uttered by me now. So the sentence 'BC is a part of Cody' is not true as uttered by me now.

Making truth relative to a frame or a foliation won't help, since according RF, ordinary objects and their temporal counterparts are 'sparse': they exactly occupy only certain select slices of the relevant paths. No BC-temporal counterpart (located in the relevant region) is a part of any Cody-temporal counterpart.

4. Conclusion

There are, of course, responses that I haven't considered. One might reject relativity. One might insist that any possible spacetime has a unique privileged foliation. One might deny the possibility of the relevant sorts of material objects.[32] My goal here has been not been to settle on any particular solution, but only to raise the puzzle and to argue that the most tempting responses to it are more problematic than they initially appear to be.[33]

Notes

1 According to stage theory, ordinary objects are instantaneous stages each of which is located at just a single, temporally unextended spacetime region (Hawley, 2001; Sider, 2001). Ordinary objects persist, on this view, by having other stages (ones that are located at earlier or later spacetime regions) as temporal counterparts. Stage theory is typically contrasted with (i) *worm theory*, according to which ordinary objects are temporally extended 'worms' that have different temporal parts located at different times/spacetime regions and with (ii) *endurantism*, according to which ordinary objects are temporally unextended things that persist by being multilocated in spacetime – in particular, by exactly occupying each in a series of temporally unextended regions. See Balashov (2011), Hawley (2010), and Haslanger (2003) for surveys.

2 The puzzle is most vivid when set up in such a way as to anthropomorphize the objects involved, but I take it to be straightforward to recast it in non-anthropomorphic terms.

3 In the present context, we can say that the *path* of an ordinary object is the region that is exactly occupied by the sum of that object and its temporal counterparts. See Balashov (2010, 27).

4 I assume that R_B is a timelike curve that is 'infinite in both directions': for any point p in R_B and any positive real number n, (i) there is a distinct point p+ in R_B, in the chronological future of p, such that proper time elapsed along R_B from p to p+ is n minutes, and (ii) there is another point p- in R_B (p-≠p+), in the chronological past of p, such that the proper time elapsed along R_B from p- to p is n minutes.

5 A *region* is any non-empty set of spacetime points. A *hyperplane* is a region R such that for some inertial frame F and some point p: (i) p is in R, and (ii) a point p* is in R iff p* is simultaneous-in-F with p. Hyperplanes are spacelike, flat, and maximal. A hyperplane H is *associated* with an inertial frame F if and only if any two points in H are simultaneous-in-F.

6 The first two definitions are straightforward relativistic analogues of definitions from Cartwright (1987, 171). The third and fourth definitions are based more loosely on Hudson (2005, 65).

7 H – R = the set of points that are in H but not in R.

8 I will sometimes shift from talking of slices of regions to slices of objects.

9 A strict total order on a set S is a transitive, asymmetric, and irreflexive relation R such that for any x and y in S, if x≠y, then either $\langle x, y\rangle \in R$ or $\langle y, x\rangle \in R$.

10 A point p* is in the *chronological* past of a point p if and only if there is a future-directed timelike curve running from p* to p – roughly, if and only if a slower-than-light signal emitted at p* could reach p. A point p* is in the *causal* past of a point p if and only if either there is a future directed timelike curve running from p* to p or there is a future-directed lightlike curve running from p* to p – roughly, if and only if a signal traveling at or below light speed emitted at p* could reach p. The chronological past of a point is a proper subset of its causal past.

11 At least, I find it natural to think of the relation associated with R_{Pr} as a very close analogue of *being absolutely earlier than*, especially given its formal properties. Admittedly, not everyone will agree, and indeed, some might ultimately see the puzzle as constituting a *reductio* of the claim that I find so natural here. (Thanks to Cord Friebe for pressing me on this.) But this result is interesting in its own right, I think.

12 One should not interpret the diagram as suggesting that any of the stages *perceive* that they are touching B. (Presumably that would require, very roughly put, that some causal signal originating at p_c gets 'processed' by the stage in question, which would seem to be ruled out by the fact that each of the stage's parts is spacelike separated from p_c.) Instead, one should think of A as knowing in advance exactly how the encounter will play out, and setting up some sort of mechanism that guarantees that the appropriate stages will have the appropriate beliefs (which might then constitute *knowledge*, though not perceptual knowledge). A non-relativistic example: if I know that my grandmother will turn 100 at a certain instant t in 2012, I might – given sufficiently advanced technology – implant a timer in my brain that will cause me to have, at precisely t, the tensed belief that I would express with the sentence 'She is exactly 100 years old right now', and (though nothing turns on this) the belief might constitute knowledge.

13 As defined by Gibson and Pooley:

P is a[n] instantaneous temporal part of O just if (i) P is a part of O, (ii) P exactly occupies a region R_P that is spacelike, [and] (iii) R_P is a maximal spacelike subregion of the path R_O of O. (2006, 163)

14 Contrast this with a 'corner slice' case (Gilmore, 2006, 211–213): four particles, arranged in line, pop into existence simultaneously with respect to their common rest frame, the inertial frame F, remain at rest, then a few minutes later pop out of existence simultaneously with respect to F. They compose a persisting molecule. Consider the worm, W, associated with this molecule, and the worms $W_1 – W_2$ associated with the four particles. Note that there are 'corner slices' in this case: hyperplanes passing through W that intersect just one of $W_1 – W_4$. The regions of intersection correspond to instantaneous temporal parts of W, but these temporal parts are 'defective'. If you are the four-particle molecule, these defective temporal parts of W are not among your temporal counterparts. See Balashov (2010, 110–116; 2011, 33–35), Donnelly (2010, 229–230), Eagle (2011), and Sattig (MS) for further discussion of the corner slice case.

15 Contrast this with a case of 'criss-crossing' stages, e.g., with diagonal lines in a flattened 'X': ><. Each diagonal might correspond to an instantaneous temporal part through the same worm (associated with different frames). But if you are one of these parts, the other one is not a future counterpart of you. Too much of it is in your past. (Nor is the other a past counterpart of you, for parallel reasons. Either it is not a counterpart of you at all, or it is what we might call a 'criss-cross counterpart' of you. In some ways it is related to you more as a 'fellow product of a fission', i.e., as a 'fission sister', than as a temporal counterpart.) See Gilmore (2006), Gilmore (2008), Gibson and Pooley (2006), and Balashov (2010) for more on criss-crossing slices.

16 This is not an 'immaculate replacement' style-case in which a thing pops out of existence and is, by complete coincidence, immediately replaced with a duplicate that is causally unrelated to the original thing. See Swoyer (1984), Zimmerman (1997), Gibson and Pooley (2006), Gilmore (2006), and Balashov (2010, 116–129).

17 For simplicity, suppose that spatially one-dimensional beings can feel pain. (The spatial one-dimensionality of the being in question is not essential to the paper. At the cost of some extra complexity, the paper could focus instead on a parallel case involving spatially three-dimensional things with the appropriate spatial topological properties.) Even so, it's not clear that a given instantaneous stage could feel extreme pain without having neighbors that feel some pain. Though nor is it clear that this case is impossible. Even if being in extreme pain is a highly relational property (Sider, 2001, 198), requiring the existence of past and future stages with appropriate intrinsic properties of their own, it doesn't follow that 'pains always build up gradually', so to speak.

18 Gibson and Pooley sketch a proposal about the truth conditions of tensed utterances that might block the case for (2) and (3):

"Here by 'moment' we mean a temporally extended but short-lived (i.e., momentary) interval, and the answer will depend upon its temporal extent. Let us first take it to be the duration of the specious present, the time it takes to have a single thought or enjoy a single experience. This, let us say, is about 0.2 of a second. Call the temporally extended spacetime region you occupy (partially or multiply) during this 'moment' *NOW*. To be something that can affect you in the NOW, an object must be located within the backward lightcone of the future boundary of the NOW. To be something that can be affected by you, as located in the NOW, the object must fall within the future light cone of the past boundary of NOW. Call the region bounded by these two lightcones the *Stein Present* of the NOW. The NOW's Stein Present is a four-dimensional discus-shaped region centered on the NOW ... Our tensed talk, which reports our spatiotemporal perspective on the world as at R, should be partially analyzed in terms of R's Stein Present. The present tense is correctly used at R to talk about objects and events as they are in the Stein present of R, the past tense is correctly used to talk about objects and events as they are in the absolute past of R [and so on for the future tense]." (2006, 165–167)

Adapting this suggestion to a stage theoretic context, the idea would be that 'I was touching someone' is not true as uttered by Stage 2, since Stage 2's NOW, R, is temporally extended in such a way that Stage 2 does not have any temporal counterparts that are both: (i) in the absolute past of R and (ii) touching someone. I cannot do justice to this interesting proposal here.

19 It has been suggested to me that if x is a non-flat spacelike stage in Minkowski spacetime, then it is somehow senseless (or at least incorrect) to say that x is *touching* something (presumably even after we modify our extant definitions in the relevant manner). The motivation for this claim, as I understand it, is that (i) touching is a spatial relation that holds only between things that exactly occupy only instantaneous spacetime regions, and (ii) the only spacetime regions that count as instantaneous in Minkowski spacetime are *subregions of hyperplanes* and hence *flat*. In response, I doubt both (i) and (ii). Against (i), I see no reason why two four-dimensional, temporally extended objects couldn't touch one another at a certain spacetime point. Presumably a worm theorist ought to say that A and B touch one another at point p_c despite they fact that they are both temporally extended things, neither of which exactly occupies an instantaneous region. Against (ii), it seems to me that 'spacelike' (or 'achronal') is a sufficiently close relativistic counterpart of 'instantaneous', even in Minkowski spacetime. But a full defense of this claim lies beyond the scope of the present paper. For further relevant discussion, see Gilmore (2006) and Gibson and Pooley (2006).

20 To see why the qualification about time travel is needed, suppose that A undergoes the encounter described by the oracle and shortly thereafter disappears, reappearing shortly prior to the collision, this time on the left side of B. The time traveling A races to catch up with B (who is moving to the right) and eventually does so, just managing to make contact with B at p_c. The time traveling A then jumps into the future and appears there

just where and when she had originally disappeared, thus leaving no gap in her path. (There are other more physically realistic ways of telling the story as well.) In this modified case, A and B make contact at just a single spacetime point, but intuitively A does seem to be in a position to say 'I am touching someone and I will be touching someone' at one moment of A's career and 'I am touching someone and I was touching someone' at another moment. A further revision, involving an additional trip back in time, would give us a case in which it plausible that A is in a position to utter the sentence considered in the main text. (These cases suggest that truth conditions for de re temporal predications should be given in terms of personal time rather than external time.)

21 Though for dissent, see Balashov (2010, 94–102). I suspect that many of the authors who make use of inertial frames and hyperplanes do so only as a matter of convenience and would, if pressed, agree that more general (but more complex) accounts are preferable. Often the more general accounts are not especially difficult to formulate and do not differ in any interesting or significant way from the simpler accounts, in which case there is little reason to bother with them. The present case, in my view, is an exception to the rule.

22 Some general relativistic spacetimes do contain inertial frames. Minkowski spacetime is a general relativistic spacetime (corresponding to one possible way in which the universe could be empty) and it contains inertial frames.

23 Given a suitably generalized (and still tenseless) notion of touching. The notion defined earlier depends upon the existence of hyperplanes. Henceforth I leave this qualification implicit.

24 Gödel (1949). See Lockwood (2003, e.g., 128–130) for helpful discussion.

25 Though some foliable spacetimes do contain CTCs, e.g., a Minkowski spacetime that is 'rolled up' in the appropriate way.

26 See Earman (1995, 171) and Gilmore (2006, 229, note 19) for details.

27 Given a suitably generalized (and still tenseless) notion of touching. The notion defined earlier depends upon the existence of hyperplanes. Henceforth I leave this qualification implicit.

28 An analogous but less specific thought is expressed by Michael Rea:

A perdurantist who believes in persisting persons will, I take it, think that there is some 'right' way to carve up a person into thought-bearing person-stages. (1998, 232–3)

In stage theoretic terms, the idea is that not just any way of slicing up the path of a given o-worm yields regions that are exactly occupied by temporal counterparts of an ordinary object: rather, only *one* such slicing does this. Likewise, an endurantist might say that not just any way of slicing up the path of a given ordinary object yields regions that are exactly occupied by the object; rather, only one foliation of the given path yields regions that are so occupied. Rea thinks that we may be unable to formulate a general principle that tells us, as applied to the case of a given object, which slicing is the privileged one.

29 See Gibson and Pooley (2006, 194–195, note 29), Balashov (2010, 191–195), and Balashov (this volume) for more on this. It is worth noting, how-

ever, that even if there are problem cases involving regions to which the notion of a rest frame foliation cannot be sensibly applied, this is not obviously fatal to RF. For it is always open to the stage theorist to hold that the problematic regions in question are ipso facto not exactly occupied by o-worms. The idea would be to adopt a relatively 'sparse' theory of ordinary objects, and to say that an object o1 counts as *ordinary* only if, among other things, the region that is exactly occupied by the o1-worm admits of a unique rest frame foliation. If the only regions that do not admit of rest frame foliations are relatively 'exotic' ones, then the present strategy would not be especially costly.

30 Unless A is accelerating *very* rapidly at the relevant moment of its career. If its acceleration is such as to make some of its rest frame slices 'converge' on a single point in the relevant way, then presumably there's nothing objectionable (only surprising) about the given sentence's being true as uttered by the given stage.

31 Here I am ignoring complications involving things that are multi-located or things that are located somewhere without exactly occupying any region. See Parsons (2007), Gilmore (2006), and Gilmore (2009).

32 This is less promising than it may sound, given the plausibility of abundant, supersubstantivalist views about material objects. According to supersubtantivalism, material objects are identical to (or mereologically coincide with) spacetime regions of certain sorts. 'Abundant' versions of supersubstantivalism say that every spacetime region is (or mereologically coincides with) a material object. (See Hawthorne (2006, viii, 118) and Schaffer (2009) for discussion.) According to such a view, if some spatially zero-dimensional timelike region is in contact with some spatially one-dimensional temporally extended region (that doesn't include its spatial endpoints) at just a single point (in the manner specified in the paper), then there are corresponding material objects that behave in the corresponding way. In the context of such a view, the most plausible way to deny the possibility of the relevant sorts of material objects is to take spacetime to be *gunky* (in the manner of Arntzenius, 2008).

33 Special thanks to Yuri Balashov, Florian Fischer, Cord Friebe, Thomas Müller, and Oliver Pooley for helpful comments.

References

Arntzenius, Frank, 2008: Gunk, Topology, and Measure. In: *Oxford Studies in Metaphysics* 4, pp. 225–247.

Balashov, Yuri, 2010: *Persistence and Spacetime*. Oxford: Oxford University Press.

Balashov, Yuri, 2011: Persistence. In: Craig Callender (ed.) *The Oxford Handbook of Time.* Oxford: Oxford University Press, pp. 13–40.

Balashov, Yuri, 2012: Do composite objects have an age in relativistic spacetime? In: *Philosophia Naturalis*, this volume.

Cartwright, Richard, 1987: *Philosophical Essays*. Cambridge: MIT.

Donnelly, Maureen, 2010: Parthood and Multilocation. In: *Oxford Studies in Metaphysics* 5, pp. 203–243.

Earman, John, 1995: *Bangs, Crunches, Wimpers, Shrieks*. Oxford: Oxford University Press.

Gibson, Ian; and Pooley, Oliver, 2006: Relativistic Persistence. In: *Philosophical Perspectives, 20, Metaphysics*, pp. 157–198.

Gilmore, Cody, 2006: Where in the Relativistic World Are We? In: *Philosophical Perspectives, 20, Metaphysics*, pp. 199–236.

Gilmore, Cody, 2008: Persistence and Location in Relativistic Spacetime. *Philosophy Compass* 3, pp. 1224–1254.

Gilmore, Cody, 2009: Why Parthood Might Be a Four-Place Relation, and How It Behaves If It Is. In: Ludger Honnefelder, Edmund Runggaldier, and Benedikt Schick (eds.) *Unity and Time in Metaphysics*. Berlin: de Gruyter, pp. 83–133.

Gödel, Kurt, 1949: A Remark about the Relationship between Relativity Theory and Idealistic Philosophy. In: P. A. Schilpp (ed.) *Albert Einstein: Philosopher-Scientist*. La Salle, IL: Open Court, pp. 557–562.

Haslanger, Sally, 2003: Persistence through Time. In Michael Loux and Dean Zimmerman (eds.) *The Oxford Handbook of Metaphysics*. Oxford: Oxford University Press, pp. 315–354.

Hawley, Katherine, 2001: *How Things Persist*. Oxford: Clarendon Press.

Hawley, Katherine, 2010: Temporal Parts. In: Edward N. Zalta (ed.): *The Stanford Encyclopedia of Philosophy* (Winter 2010 Edition), URL = http://plato.stanford.edu/archives/win2010/entries/temporal-parts/.

Hawthorne, John, 2006: *Metaphysical Essays*. Oxford: Oxford University Press.

Hudson, Hud, 2005: *The Metaphysics of Hyperspace*. Oxford: Oxford University Press.

Lockwood, Michael, 2003: *The Labyrinth of Time*. Oxford: Oxford University Press.

Rea, Michael, 1998: Temporal Parts Unmotivated. In: *The Philosophical Review* 107, pp. 225–260.

Sattig, Thomas. MS. 'Ordinary Objects in the Relativistic World'.

Schaffer, Jonathan, 2009: Spacetime the One Substance. In: *Philosophical Studies* 145, pp. 131–147.

Sider, Theodore, 2001: *Four Dimensionalism: An Ontology of Persistence and Time*. Oxford: Oxford University Press.

Swoyer, Chris, 1984: Causation and Identity. In: Peter French, Theodore E. Uehling, Jr., and Howard Wettstein (eds.) *Midwest Studies in Philosophy* 9. Minneapolis, MN: U of Minnesota P, pp. 593–622.

Zimmerman, Dean, 1997: Immanent Causation. In: *Philosophical Perspectives, 11, Mind, Causation, and World*, pp. 433–71.

Thomas Müller

Indeterminism and persistence

Abstract

This paper aims at bringing together two debates in metaphysics that so far have been kept separate: the debate about determinism vs. indeterminism as *de re* modality on the one hand, and the debate about persistence on the other hand. Both debates significantly involve talk of things. We will show that working out a proper semantics for singular terms and an accompanying theory of things, motivated by considerations of quantified modal logic, can significantly further the persistence debate. We will use our semantic framework to give an argument in support of the endurantist (3-dimensionalist) position as the best theory of persistence.

Zusammenfassung

Das Ziel dieses Aufsatzes ist es, zwei metaphysische Debatten miteinander zu verbinden, die bislang unverbunden nebeneinander stehen: die Debatte um Determinismus und Indeterminsmus im Sinne von Möglichkeit *de re* einerseits, und die Persistenzdebatte andererseits. In beiden Debatten spielt die Rede von Dingen eine wichtige Rolle. Es wird gezeigt, dass eine adäquate, durch Überlegungen zur quantifizierten Modallogik motivierte Semantik für singulare Terme und eine damit verbundene Theorie von Dingen die Persistenzdebatte deutlich voranbringen kann. Im Rahmen unserer Theorie geben wir ein Argument für Endurantismus (Dreidimensionalismus) als beste Theorie von Persistenz.

1. Introduction

The metaphysical debate about the determinism or indeterminism of the world we live in (only one possible future, or many?), is hardly ever mentioned when it comes to the metaphysical question of how things persist (how a thing can remain the same through changes in the course of time). We believe that this points to a blind spot in the debate, rather than conceptual independence, and that a combination of both debates can lead to new insights for the question of persistence. We will argue that the connection should be forged via an appropriate semantics for singular terms that refer to things: the phenomena of persistence and *de re* modality call for the same semantical approach.

Prima facie, it doesn't seem too far-fetched to expect some interaction between the questions of determinism and persistence, as both questions are about the temporal development of the world around us and the things in it. To be precise, the question of determinism would also arise in a world (unlike ours) in which there are no things, but just, e.g., a single field with a changing state. We will however assume that we are dealing with a world in which there are things. On that basis, we immediately have a sufficient condition for indeterminism: if there is one thing in the world that can persist in more than one way (one thing that has open possibilities for its future), then the world is indeterministic. (Depending on how strongly one reads the assumption that we are dealing with a world of things, this condition may also be necessary for indeterminism.)

So, here is a first link: any unrealized possibility of a persisting thing (an unrealized possibility *de re*) is sufficient for indeterminism. We may safely assume that any of the normal things around us is a witness for indeterminism in that sense. Surely, e.g., the glass of water on the table before me can persist until tomorrow or be destroyed today: two incompatible possibilities for its future development, only one of which will be realized.[1]

This link between indeterminism and persistence can hardly be denied, but it may also seem rather trivial.[2] It is less clear whether the fact of indeterminism (assuming, together with common sense, that it *is* a fact) also teaches us something interesting about persistence.[3] Given that there are things facing more than one possible future development (and, to repeat, it is hard to deny that all things around us are like that), the following question arises: Which implications does this have for the persistence debate? Is the fact that there are numerous non-trivial *de re* possibilities for things, of any help in deciding the thorny question of *how things persist*?

Recall that in the recent persistence debate, there are three rival accounts, one three-dimensionalist theory, *endurance*, and two four-dimensionalist theories, *perdurance* and *exdurance*. According to the endurantist view, a normal thing is a three-dimensional entity that persists (remains the same through changes) "by being wholly present at more than one time":[4] probably the best sense one can make of this is: at each moment of its existence, it is present with all of its parts.[5] Endurantism is the commonsensical view; the main challenge for endurantism, the problem of change, is to explain how one and the same thing can have different (intrinsic) properties (at different moments). The four-dimensionalist approach to persistence is motivated by the conviction that the problem of change is insurmountable. According to the perdurantist view, which avoids this problem, a thing is a four-dimensional entity that persists in the sense that there are different temporal parts, or stages, of the thing, at different times. These stages are themselves different things, and it is unproblematic that they can have different intrinsic properties. The normal thing itself is, according to that view, a four-dimensional "space-time worm", which is not wholly present at any one time. Exdurantism is also a four-dimensionalist theory; however, in contrast to perdurantism, exdurantism takes the normal things we deal with to be stages and not space-time worms. Again, the problem of change is avoided as different stages can of course have different intrinsic properties. In a sense, exdurantism denies our normal conception of persistence: normal things according to exdurantism are just stages, and stages do not persist. Exdurantism, however, posits a temporal counterpart relation between stages to account for our normal talk of persistence, much like a counterpart-theoretic account of modality *de re*, and in this sense, it is still a theory of persistence (see Sider, 2001).

Our main question will be: can the phenomenon of indeterminism, as witnessed by non-trivial *de re* modality, contribute anything to the debate about persistence? We will approach this question indirectly, from a semantic perspective: we will argue for a useful semantics for singular terms that does justice to *de re* modality, and we will ask about the impact of that framework if transformed to a temporal setting. It will turn out that all three mentioned theories of persistence can be modeled in our proposed framework, which we take to be good news in favour of the neutrality of our approach. In terms of metaphysics, we take this result to favour endurantism as the commonsensical view: in metaphysics as in dealing with other complex matters, it is good methodology to subscribe to the principle "if it ain't broke, don't fix it" (Lowe, 2009, 91), and so we should stick to what we started from.

Before we begin with our semantical investigation, we need to comment on another discussion in the vicinity of our subject matter, viz., the debate between a presentist A-theory of time and an eternalist B-theory.[6] This is a thorny issue; there is even a substantial debate over whether there is a substantial debate between A-and B-theory at all (Meyer, 2005; Savitt, 2006). However that may be, it is clear that there is a significant difference at least in outlook on the status of a semantic framework, which is relevant for our enterprise. A truly presentist semantics, such as envisaged by Prior (1968), will have to treat semantics ultimately hermeneutically: our presentist natural language can only be elucidated by use of that same language (see Müller, 2007). Formal semantics is however mostly treated model-theoretically, implying a stance "above" the language to be modeled and the material it talks about; from such a stance, a whole semantic model, and thus, all of (space-)time, has to be accessible. Model-theoretic semantics is therefore essentially B-theoretic. In line with Prior, we acknowledge the power of model-theoretic methods in semantics, and we will proceed using a standard model-theoretic outlook, but we do not take this to settle the A vs. B debate in favour of B-theory; on the contrary, we want to let the A-theoretic position stand as a live option. (We do not even want to take a stance on whether ultimately there *is* a substantial issue between A-and B-theory.) Our reason for proceeding in a B-theoretic setting is purely pragmatic: it is simply much easier to formulate semantic assumptions model-theoretically.[7]

Here is how we will proceed. We start by discussing the phenomenological basis of our enterprise in § 2. In § 3, we lay out our semantic framework in detail, using mainly the phenomenon of *de re* modality and considerations of quantified modal logic as the underlying motivation. Then, in § 4, we apply the framework to the persistence debate and give our argument in favour of endurance as the best theory of persistence.

2. The phenomena of persistence and *de re* modality

Both indeterminism in the sense of *de re* modality and persistence are phenomena involving *things*. What is that: a thing? There is much debate about this notion in metaphysics. While we cannot hope to resolve the issue, a discussion of the notion of a thing will certainly be helpful to motivate our semantic framework. We will therefore proceed with the aim of fixing a notion of a thing that identifies the right sort of entity for the phenomena of persistence and *de re* modality.

We use singular terms to refer to things. This cat, my daughter's cat Hannibal, is such a thing; I can refer to him, for example, by pointing to him now, or via the singular terms "this cat" (as used now), or "Hannibal". (I can also refer-to-him-and-stroke-him, which he likes.) Hannibal, the cat I'm referring to, wouldn't be a cat if he didn't have a certain history typical of cats – he was born of a cat, and he grew up from a small, blind newborn kitten to become quite a hunter. Hannibal has a history; he also has a huge number of *de re* modal properties, forming what we may call his modal profile. He's inside now, but he could be outside now as well; he left some of his food in the bowl, but he could have eaten it all. He could not, however, turn into a dog or a butterfly. He can persist in many different ways, but not in all imaginable ways. There are distinct *de re* possibilities open for him, and his persistence is constrained in many ways, given that he is a cat.

This is the phenomenological basis from which we will start. At least the central cases in which questions of *de re* modality and persistence make sense, involve proper things, things of a specific kind. We should be happy if we can lay out a theory of persistence that is able to handle these clear cases appropriately and that gives a (hopefully illuminating) verdict on less clear cases. It would be asking too much, however, if we were looking for a theory of indeterminism and persistence that is geared towards just anything we can refer to. In order to elucidate the notion of a (proper) thing further, we need to provide a useful semantics for singular terms.

3. Establishing a useful semantics for singular terms

3.1 Extension vs. intension

Many semantic frameworks, from Frege to Montague and beyond, distinguish between two aspects of pieces of language: their *extension* and their *intension*. It is commonly acknowledged, for example, that while the predicates "animal which has a heart" and "animal which has a liver" specify the same extension (they are true of the same animals), still they specify that extension in different ways; it could be, one thinks, that the extensions are different.[8] According to Frege, who generalizes such considerations, even a sentence has an extension (a truth value) and an intension (a thought or proposition).[9] Frege's student Carnap proposes an even more general, regimented use of the extension-intension distinction. According to him, we should strive for a semantic theory in which each separate piece of language has an extension and an intension, where the intension is now a function specifying all possible extensions (the extensions in all possible cases). Carnap calls this "the method of extension and intension" (see Carnap, 1947, Ch. I).

Inspired by Carnap, Bressan (1972) suggests a fully symmetrical use of the extension/intension idea, which does away with the idea, still present in Carnap, that each piece of language has an extension *simpliciter*. According to Bressan, in many applications the possible cases (represented by a set of cases Γ) should all be treated as equally basic, as far as logic is concerned. Belnap has accordingly suggested to call that framework *case-intensional semantics*.[10] The main idea is that each piece of language ξ has an extension $ext_\gamma(\xi)$ in each case $\gamma \in \Gamma$, and its intension $int(\xi)$ is simply the corresponding function from cases to extensions:

$$ext_\gamma(\xi)=(int(\xi))(\gamma); \qquad int(\xi)=\lambda\gamma(ext_\gamma(\xi)).$$

At the ground level of the logical framework, there is no longer a suggestion that we must, or even should, distinguish a "real case" from other "merely possible" cases: the framework is fully symmetrical with respect to the cases. This will be important for our employment of the framework below.

3.2 Singular terms: extension and intension

There is a substantial debate whether it is useful to apply the extension/intension distinction to singular terms; the most hotly debated question is whether we can assume that proper names have an intension in any useful sense. From the point of view of case-intensional semantics, this question has an easy answer: as far as logic is concerned, we should start with the extension/intension distinction quite generally; principles restricting the generality of the framework should be introduced, and argued for, at the level of science or metaphysics, but not at the level of logic or semantics. Like any other piece of language, a singular term α therefore has both an intension $int(\alpha)$, and an extension

$ext_\gamma(\alpha) = (int(\alpha))(\gamma)$ in each case $\gamma \in \Gamma$. As a background assumption for the framework, there has to be, beside the set of cases Γ, a domain of extensions, D, so that $ext_\gamma(\alpha) \in D$.[11]

3.3 Identity and predication

As a next step in giving an overview of the framework, it is useful to see how predication and identity statements are handled in case-intensional semantics. First, some pertinent terminology: we call a predicate P *extensional* if the question whether $P\alpha$ holds in a case γ, for α any singular term, can be answered solely on the basis of the *extension* of α in case γ, $ext_\gamma(\alpha)$. Predicates that are not extensional are called *intensional*; they look, as it were, beyond a given single case. The basic slogan for case-intensional semantics in this respect is "identity is extensional, predication is intensional". That is, the basic semantic resources for predication allow for intensional predication, while the basic semantic resources for identity statements are purely extensional.

Put formally, this means that an identity statement "$\alpha = \beta$", with α and β singular terms, is true in case γ iff $ext_\gamma(\alpha) = ext_\gamma(\beta)$; thus, it is true or false solely on the basis of the extensions of the terms involved.[12] A predicate P, on the other hand, is treated as a piece of language with an extension $ext_\gamma(P)$ in each case γ, and a corresponding intension $int(P)$. What is the extension of a predicate? There are two obvious choices. If one wants predication to be extensional, as in first-order logic, then one will assign a subset of the domain D as the extension of a one-place predicate: $ext_\gamma(P) \subseteq D$. P then applies to α in case γ iff $ext_\gamma(\alpha) \in ext_\gamma(P)$. The more general choice, adopted in the framework of case-intensional semantics, is to treat predication as intensional in each case. That is, the extension of a predicate P in a case γ, $ext_\gamma(P)$, sorts not extensions (members of D), but individual intensions (functions from Γ to D) into those to which the predicate applies in the given case and those to which it doesn't. In this way, predication *in a case* can still look further than that particular case: predication is basically intensional. Extensional predicates turn out to be a special case: a predicate P is extensional in case γ if and only if, if $P\alpha$ and $\alpha = \beta$ in that case, then also $P\beta$.

Although extensional predication is a special case logically speaking, it is the usual case from a pragmatic point of view: a large number of important predicates are extensional. Our chief use of non-extensional predicates is in connection with sorts of things (see § 3.8 below).

3.4 *Modality*

In case-intensional semantics, it is rather straightforward to implement modal operators for possibility and necessity. Instead of the usual slogan of modal logic, "necessity is truth in all (accessible) possible worlds", which triggers a metaphysics of possible worlds as wholly separate but mutually accessible entities, of which we should be suspicious, we can use a metaphysically neutral slogan that is also idiomatic English: something is necessary if it is true in any case. Dually, something is possible if it is true in some (possible) case.[13]

As usually, the modal operators are written as "□" ("necessarily") and "◊" ("possibly"), and we can treat "◊" as an abbreviation for "¬□¬". The semantics of "□" is given by universal quantification over cases: $\Box\phi$ is true in a case γ iff ϕ is true in all cases $\gamma' \in \Gamma$. Note that unlike in standard Kripke semantics for modal logic, here no relation of accessibility is needed, and the modal system is therefore simply S5.

Now we have a notion of modality; does this help us to spell out modality *de re*? As argued above, we are looking for modality *de re* in a literal sense: modality of things. So we need to have a good look at the interrelation of singular terms and things in order to understand *de re* modality. We start by looking at so-called "empty" singular terms.

3.5 *Singular terms: "empty" terms*

It is a well known fact, which has given rise to a lot of semantic effort, that some syntactically well-formed singular terms "misbehave": they do not single out anything. In our framework, we can already make a distinction at that point: among the so-called "empty" or "non-referring" singular terms, there are some, like "the odd prime", which do not single out anything in any case; they are, so to speak, completely empty. The most famous example of an "empty" singular term, Russell's (1905) example of "the present king of France", is however interestingly different: it does not single out any person now, but it did in earlier times. If cases are temporal (we will come to that below in §4), we can say that "the present king of France" singles out somebody in some (earlier) cases, but not now (in the present case, as it were).

There are several ways to deal with this phenomenon of emptyness, from Russell's much-discussed move of treating definite descriptions as incomplete symbols to be eliminated in context, to systems of free logic. We go for a simple treatment of these phenomena, along Frege's lines:

we will use a "throwaway" entity $N \in D$ to handle lack of extension in a case. Thus, if $ext_\gamma(\alpha) = N$, this signals that α does not exist in case γ. Accordingly, we can define an (extensional) existence predicate, E: $E\alpha$ holds in case γ iff $ext_\gamma(\alpha) \neq$ N.[14]

We put "empty" in scare-quotes for a reason. As stated, the term "the present king of France" hasn't always failed to single out some person – France was a monarchy for quite some time. We normally call a term "empty" because it fails to single out anything *now*, in what we may want to call "the real case". We already said that from the logical point of view of case-intensional semantics, we are not committed to the existence of a "real case". Whether there is a "real case", and thus an extension of a term *simpliciter*, depends on the metaphysics of the specific framework at hand, i.e., on the metaphysical status of the cases in Γ. In standard modal logic, the "actual world" (in the sense of: the world of a context of utterance) can be taken to be the "real case"; in linear tense logic, the present time (the time of the context of utterance) will supply a "real case". But not all case-intensional frameworks have to be like that.[15] Keeping the semantics symmetrical with respect to the cases is important for a useful, general semantic framework.

3.6 Singular terms: reference

What does a singular term refer to? Above (§ 2) we commented on our everyday assumption about using singular terms: the *referent* of a singular term such as "this cat" is a *thing* – that which has a history, and which has properties, including *de re* modal properties. How does this connect with the case-intensional semantic framework?

The standard way to specify a semantics for singular terms, even in intensional logics, is firmly rooted in classical predicate logic. Given a world, a time, or another suitable set of parameters of truth (a case, as we would say), a domain of objects is singled out, and the referent of a singular term is taken to be one of the objects in that domain. There is much discussion about the domains (e.g., whether they are constant across different cases), but the basic assumption is that a domain is a domain of things. In our terminology, this would mean that the extensional domain D is viewed as a domain of things, and that the extension of a singular term in a case is one of the things from the domain. Together with the common assumption about the referent of singular terms, this would mean that the referent of a term in a case (the thing referred to in that case) is its extension in that case – and in fact, it is common to use "referent" synonymously with "extension".

We hold that the tradition of predicate logic is pushing in an unhelpful direction here. Recall that predicate logic was invented initially to deal with difficulties in the foundations of mathematics: a science of timeless, immutable objects like sets and numbers – no questions of *de re* modality, no questions of persistence. It is clear that the logical framework of predicate logic has to be extended to account for these more worldly phenomena. Should we hold on to the assumption of a domain of things? It is the common thing to do, for systems of quantified modal logic as well as for systems of temporal logic. In case-intensional logic, however, it will not do: extensions can't be things, and our domain D cannot be a domain of things.

It is perhaps best to establish this for the case of *de re* modality, where the cases $\gamma \in \Gamma$ are possible cases in some adequate sense of possibility (no ontology of "possible worlds" has to be presupposed). This way, we will have an independent background for transferring our semantic insights to the temporal case that is the main objective of this paper. Our consideration is similar to Kripke's famous Humphrey objection to Lewis (Kripke, 1980, 45n13), but with a twist that should make it less debatable. Consider a thing that is red, but that could be green. Fairly idiomatically we can rephrase this as follows: the thing is red in the case at hand, but it could be green in another case. In case-intensional semantics this means that the extensional predicate "... is red" applies in the case at hand, γ_1, but not in some other case, γ_2: $R\alpha$ is true in case γ_1, but $\Diamond\neg R\alpha$ is true there as well (where R stands for the predicate "... is red" and α is a name of the thing in question). The predicate "... is red" being extensional, this means that the extension of α in γ_1, $ext_y(\alpha)$, differs from the extension of α in γ_2, $ext_{\gamma_2}(\alpha)$, in such a way that "... is red" applies in the one case but not in the other. But this just means that the extension *cannot* be the thing in question. There is, by assumption, just one thing, which is red in one case and green in another. This thing can't be identical to an extension in a case, since the extensions in the cases γ_1 and γ_2 have to be different in order for an extensional predicate, like "... is red", to apply to one and not to the other.

This consideration was based on extensional predication. Intensional predication gives an additional argument. In our framework, an extension is something confined to a single case (something that can exist at such a case). If we allow for intensional predication, then in a sentence such as $P\alpha$, the singular term α must refer to the thing, not the extension in a case – otherwise, the intension of P and the referent of α wouldn't be enough to give a compositional account of the truth or falsity of $P\alpha$ in a case at hand. The upshot is that an individual term α should be taken to *refer to the individual intension* $int(\alpha)$, not the extension $ext_\gamma(\alpha)$ at a given case γ.

We can strengthen this verdict by looking at singular terms in more detail. So far, there has been no restriction on the singular terms and their interpretation at all: anything goes, including the empty extension at any number of cases. In our framework, the throwaway entity N is the extension not only for failing definite descriptions like "the present king of France" (in the present case) or "the odd prime" (in all cases), but also for regular terms, like proper names, in cases in which the named object or person simply does not exist. In this respect, "the present king of France" isn't very much different from "Socrates": both specify an individual intension, and for both, the extension is empty in the present case, but nonempty in earlier cases.[16] "Socrates" isn't an empty name – it refers; it is just that at present, its extension is empty. Note that even "the odd prime" has an associated individual intension; it is however empty in all cases, represented as the constant function that assigns the throwaway extension N to all cases. Here we may say that it is a merely technical fact that that singular term refers, whereas in fact we have failure of reference: the fact that there is a referent, is "implementation dependent" as it were, depending on our choice to represent failure of a definite description in a case via assigning the "empty extension", which in turn is represented by an element N of the domain D.

For another example of the (potential) "anything goes" of our framework, take the singular term "Peter's favourite object". This may have been a soft toy when he was two, a bike later on, then something he got from his girlfriend, or his phone. No matter: the intension of that term is simply some individual intension, a function from Γ to D. (Quite plausibly we should take the extension of that term to be N in all those cases γ in which Peter himself doesn't exist, i. e., in which $ext_\gamma(\text{Peter}) = N$.) Of course, the resources of natural language for specifying individual intensions are limited, but in principle, *any* function from Γ to D could be the intension of some term, and thus could be referred to. Any individual intension can be an *object of reference*.

3.7 *Quantifiers*

We have argued that singular terms refer to individual intensions, while their extensions are case-specific. Variables being singular terms as well, this has consequences for the interpretation of quantification: the quantifiers in our framework range over all possible individual intensions. Thus, in a technical development of first-order case-intensional semantics, we will need an assignment for the variables that specifies one individual intension per variable, and the quantifiers will change that assignment as usual, replacing the appropriate individual intension by another.[17]

Can we read these quantifiers in the usual way then, as "for at least one thing x" ($\exists x$) and "for all things x" ($\forall x$)? This seems doubtful. Consider Peter's favourite object again. Even leaving to the side the cases in which there is no extension for that term, that "object" behaves strangely. It does not make sense to inquire into "its" persistence, even though the "object" surely has different properties at different times (for example, "it" is big and fluffy in an earlier case, but small and hard now). It makes no good sense either to ask about its *de re* modal properties, even though "it" could be red, or yellow, or green. The term "Peter's favourite object" certainly specifies an *object of reference,* like any singular term. "Peter's favourite object" however doesn't specify a *proper thing.*

It is proper things, though, that we normally care about, and whose *de re* modality and persistence we are trying to understand. This comes out nicely in a double reading of the quantifiers, which does *not* coincide with the purported difference of "possibilist" vs. "actualist" quantification that is much discussed in quantified modal logic. What about the sentence

There is something that is Peter's favourite object,

uttered in a case γ? Taking π to abbreviate the singular term "Peter's favourite object", the sentence seems to have the form "$\exists x x = \pi$", which is trivially true according to our semantics for the quantifiers (we can just assign to x the intension of π). There is however a more interesting reading, which stresses the "thing" in "something": in case γ, there is a *proper thing* that is (in that case) identical with Peter's favourite object,

$$\exists x\ (PTx\ \&\ x = \pi).$$

Here we use "*PT*" to stand for the (intensional) predicate of objects of reference, "being a proper thing", to be elucidated in § 3.8 below.

The distinction between objects of reference and proper things is made even more explicit when one tries to force a *de re* reading for "Peter's favourite object". The natural interpretation for a sentence expressing a *de re* possibility, such as

Of Peter's favourite object it is true that it could be green,

is that there is a *proper thing* (e.g., one of his model trains), which in fact (in the case at hand) is Peter's favourite object, and of which the *de re* modal attribution is true. The fact that Peter's favourite object could be something else which in fact is green (i.e., that there is a case in which the extension of "Peter's favourite object" satisfies the extensional predicate "... is green"), does not seem enough to make the displayed *de re* sentence true. In the same vein, it does make sense to inquire into the persistence of the proper thing that is actually (in a given case) Peter's favourite object, but not to ask how Peter's favourite thing, considered as an object of reference, persists.

It is at this semantic level that questions of indeterminism (in the form of *de re* modality) and persistence come together.

3.8 Characterizing proper things

So far, the individual intension $int(\alpha)$ of a singular term α is our technical representation of an *object of reference.* Any function from Γ to D can constitute such an object of reference. In line with our interest in *de re* modality and persistence, however, we are mostly interested in *proper things*, such as cats, pine trees, tables or cups.[18] It is their persistence that a theory of persistence should explain, and their *de re* modal properties that a theory of *de re* modality should illuminate. It would be asking too much, or indeed the wrong thing, if we were aiming at a fully general theory of modality and persistence for *objects of reference.* When asked about the persistence of a thing whose extension in different cases picks out Julius Caesar, the moon, a piece of chalk and a frog (and maybe that *is* Peter's favourite object), we should simply deny that such a "thing", even if we can refer to it, persists in any meaningful way, or that we understand what is meant when we hear that *it* could be green.

It should be clear now that this development of objects of reference as individual intensions is different from the standard way of analytic metaphysics, which would probably construe a general notion of an object as a mereological sum of temporal parts of ordinary things, if these are acknowledged, or just as (the contents of) a region of space-time. No temporal parts are invoked in our development. Apart from a leaner ontology, this also means that we can leave the original notion of a part intact, so that for proper things, "part" just means "spatial part".

How can we distinguish mere objects of reference from proper things? In our framework, we take a lead from the idea that a proper thing falls under a sortal: we characterize proper things semantically by way of characterizing sortal predicates. This idea certainly has a (neo-)Aristotelian ring to it, but we endorse the thought that "a view is not necessarily wrong because Aristotle held it" (Prior, 1967a, 10).[19]

It is difficult to determine what the proper sortal predicates are. At the level of abstraction of this paper, we can leave that open (see note 18). We will simply assume that there is an (intensional) predicate of predicates, *Sortal*, such that F is a sortal predicate iff *Sortal* (F) is true.[20] Some useful assumptions about *Sortal* are the following:

- If *Sortal* (F) and α is a singular term, then if there is a case in which a exists and falls under F (i.e., if it is true that $\Diamond(E\alpha \;\&\; F\alpha)$), then α falls under F in all cases in which it exists ($\Box(E\alpha \rightarrow F\alpha)$). Once a cat, always a cat. Bressan calls this "quasi-modal constancy"; the "quasi" comes in because nonexistence at some cases is allowed for. This principle encodes our commonsensical idea that transsubstantiation doesn't occur: if we have correctly specified the sortal under which something falls, then that sortal will stick, as it were, for life.[21]
- If *Sortal* (F) and α and β are singular terms, then if there is a case in which α and β exist, both β fall under F, and they coincide in that case ($\Diamond(E\alpha \;\&\; F\alpha \;\&\; F\beta \;\&\; \alpha = \beta)$), then α and β are identical in all cases, i.e., they fully coincide ($\Box(\alpha = \beta)$). There is thus *no overlap between things of the same sort*. No two cats in the same place. Note that this leaves it open that there might be overlap in the sense that, for example, there is both a statue and a lump of clay constituting the statue at the same place, even though they are not identical: two different proper things of different sorts might very well have the same extension in one case.[22]

Bressan calls this principle "quasi-modal separation"; together with modal constancy, we have specified his notion of "quasi-absoluteness". Belnap and Müller (2012) drop the "quasi".

We do not take a stance here as to whether *Sortal* is fully characterized via absoluteness – ultimately this will depend on the set of cases Γ under consideration, and an informal notion of naturalness may have to be invoked in addition. At least it should be clear that our framework has the resources to spell out the logical aspects of the predicate *Sortal* in as much detail as is needed.

A proper thing is, then, an object of reference (an individual intension) that falls under a sortal. Thus,

$$PT(\alpha) \Leftrightarrow \exists F\,(Sortal\,(F)\ \&\ F\alpha).$$

Let us see how this works out in the case of the cat, Hannibal. (We will discuss the appropriate set of cases Γ in §4 below; here we simply take cases to be times.) *Cat* is a sortal; *Sortal(Cat)* is true in any case. We abbreviate the singular term, "Hannibal", as "*h*". To say that Hannibal is a cat, is to apply the intensional predicate *Cat*, which "looks beyond" any particular case. Cats have cat-histories; things that have different histories, even if they momentarily were to look like a cat, aren't cats. There is pretty widespread consensus about this role of a thing's history for its belonging to a sort; for two rather different views agreeing on this, see, e.g., the swampman thought experiment by Davidson (1987), and Thompson (2003). Given our present distinction between objects of reference and proper things, we can support this position in the following way. Let the singular term "*c*" have as its referent a proper thing different from Hannibal, say a teacup. There are, therefore, individual intensions *int*(*c*) and *int(h)* that represent the cup and the cat, respectively, and that fully specify their histories. Now define the individual intension $\Im$ as follows:

$$\Im(\gamma) = \begin{cases} (int(h))(\gamma) & \text{for } \gamma = t_\circ, \\ (int(c))(\gamma) & \text{for } \gamma \neq t_\circ. \end{cases}$$

Let "Hcup" be a singular term that has the individual intension $\Im$ as its object of reference. (No problem; maybe *that* is Peter's favourite object.) In case $t_\circ$, i.e., locally to case $t_\circ$, this object of reference has, by assumption, the same extension as "Hannibal" in that case: $ext_{t_\circ}(h) = (int(h))$

$(t_0) = \Im(t_0) = ext_{t_0}$ ("Hcup"). Accordingly, in case t_0, "Hcup = h" is true; it is impossible to distinguish Hcup from Hannibal by focusing on case t_0 alone. It would however be wrong to say that Hcup is a cat: it clearly isn't; any other case will show this. And even if we change the definition of $\Im$ to

$$\Im(\gamma) = \begin{cases} (int(h))(\gamma) & \text{for } \gamma \geq t_0, \\ (int(c))(\gamma) & \text{for } \gamma < t_0. \end{cases}$$

which may be a more appropriate candidate for Peter's favourite object, what we get is not a cat, but something like a swamp-cat: something that, even though it may forever be indistinguishable from a cat after t_0, isn't a cat since it doesn't have a cat's history. In order to see whether some object of reference (an individual intension) is a proper thing of a specific sort, one needs to look further than any given case. Sortal predication, and therefore the notion of a proper thing, is highly intensional.

4. Moments as cases: a case-intensional discussion of persistence

We haven't been precise so far in specifying what our set of cases Γ should be for a proper discussion of proper things and their indeterminism and persistence. Accordingly, we have left it vague what we take to be the extensions in D. In line with the overall aim of our paper, now is the time to commit.

We hold that ultimately, a realistic environment for the discussion of indeterminism and persistence will have to be based on cases in branching time or, more adequately, in branching space-time. These frameworks pose technical challenges that we need not discuss here. It will be sufficient to give a temporal reading to Γ and to discuss the question of persistence independently of the question of *de re* modality, simply assuming the case-intensional semantic framework that was motivated by these two phenomena together.

Our cases are therefore temporal; we can take them to be moments. Thus, a term will have an extension at any given moment; the "throwaway" extension N will represent the fact that the term in question has no extension at a given moment. An individual intension will accordingly be a function from moments to extensions. Again, things, the referents of singular terms, which have a history, are properly represented by the intensions, not the extensions: the referent of a singular term, an object of reference, is an individual intension, a function from moments to extensions.

What are these extensions? This question is of course important for our semantics, but also for its interpretation vis-à-vis the persistence debate. In a given case (at a given time), the extension of a term will have to be something that "fits" into the case; it cannot as it were extend beyond that case (see § 3.6 above). Given the fact that cases are momentary points of time, an extension therefore has to be something that is not temporally extended. This makes it plausible to take the extensions to be either stages, or states, of things. We go for the former. Note that, as laid out above, the extensions, i.e., the stages, are *not* themselves things. Our semantic choice for stages as extensions does not commit us to the existence of Stages as proper things. It *may be* (in the neutral sense of: "the framework does not exclude" – see note 22) that there are Stages: proper things that only exist in a single case, so that we may, in some weak and potentially confusing sense, identify them with their one non-trivial extension. We take this to be a broadly empirical question, which we refrain from addressing here.

Now let us move closer to the question of persistence: we want to model the true fact that Hannibal once was a kitten, but isn't any longer. In order to keep things simple, we will not speak about a cat being a kitten or not in a given case *(kitten* is a phased sortal predicate, which has intensional semantics again); rather, we will use the extensional predicate of *weighing more than 1 kg, K*. In order to model the fact that Hannibal the cat once was a kitten, weighing less than or equal to 1 kg ($\neg K(h)$ in case m_1), and now weighs more than 1 kg ($K(h)$ in case m_2), we have to have, minimally, the two cases m_1 and m_2 ($\Gamma = \{m_1, m_2\}$) and two extensions $c_1 \neq N$ and $c_2 \neq N$, cat-stages if you wish (so, including the throwaway, $D = \{N, c_1, c_2\}$). The individual intension that h refers to, $\mathfrak{I}$, is the function mapping m_1 to c_1 and m_2 to c_2. This individual intension we take to fall under the extension of the sortal predicate *Cat* at all cases (remember modal constancy, § 3.8).

Being of a real sort (being a cat), Hannibal persists, and so it makes sense to ask how his persistence is reflected in our framework. It turns out that our framework is sufficiently neutral to allow an interpretation in terms of either endurance, perdurance, or exdurance. We look at the three contenders in turn.

Endurantism. Hannibal exists at each of the two cases in question: h has a nonempty extension there ($\Im(m_1) \neq N$; $\Im(m_2) \neq N$). To say that it is one and the same cat that weighs less than 1kg in one case (at m_1) and not in another case (at m_2), is to say that the *referent* of the singular term h is *the same individual intension* $\Im$ (the same function from cases to extensions), independently of the case. The difference in the application of the (extensional) predicate K is due to the *different extensions* at the two cases. Hannibal is, if you wish, "wholly present" in both cases: he has a non-empty extension at both m_1 and at m_2, and none of his parts is missing in any case. The extensions are three-dimensional stages, but crucially, they are *not* cats, nor any other proper things, nor are they temporal parts of a cat: cats have tails, paws etc. as their spatial parts, but no temporal parts.

This appears to be a simple, coherent account of what is going on, without any need for revision.

Perdurantism. For the perdurantist, there is no important distinction between extension and referent. The extension of the term h is a space-time worm; in our simple model, this amounts to taking the extension of h to be the graph of the function $\Im$, represented, for example, by the set that has as elements the pairs $\langle m_1, c_1 \rangle$ and $\langle m_2, c_2 \rangle$. To say that Hannibal weighed less than 1 kg in case m_1 is to say, on that view, that there is a *temporal part* of the space-time worm (of the graph), which is a thing itself, that weighs less than 1 kg; in our example, this will be the stage at m_1, c_1. Another temporal part of the worm, c_2, is heavier. This is extensional predication. Intensional predication can be accounted for as well: it can be read as predication of the whole worm.

From the point of view of case-intensional semantics, this reading is similar to endurantism – what a singular term *refers* to is rather similar in both cases (the function vs. its graph). Endurantism, as the home theory of case-intensional semantics, however also speaks about *extensions at cases:* the values of the intension-function, which are extensional entities that are themselves *not* things. Perdurantism, in comparison, trades a merely semantic phenomenon – the difference between the extension of a term in a case and its intensional reference – for a metaphysical theory of temporal parts of things, which themselves have to be yet more things. This appears to be unnecessarily revisionistic. Once the semantics is clarified, there is no need for the ontological move implied by perdurantism any more.

Exdurantism. Exdurantism, as proposed by Sider (1996, 2001), collapses extensions and referents in the other direction: according to that view, the term *h* refers to its endurantist extension in a given case, which is a stage. All predication therefore has to be extensional – there simply is nothing over and above the extensions to predicate anything of. A temporal counterpart relation is needed in order to bind together the various extensions to form something like a persisting thing.

This view nicely captures the extensional aspects of our endurantist theory, but it falls short of the intensional aspects. These all need to be simulated by means of a counterpart relation. Therefore, exdurantism is also highly revisionistic, taking us to be referring to momentarily existing, instantaneously vanishing entities when we think we are referring to, e.g., a cat as something that has a history.

There is no need to go along with this type of revisionism once we see that the semantic basis that allows a complicated reading in terms of exdurantism, also allows for a perfectly simple reading in terms of endurantism.

5. Conclusion

We have used the phenomena of indeterminism, in the sense of *de re* modality, and persistence, to motivate the semantical framework of case-intensional semantics, which allows a detailed characterization of the proper things to which indeterminism and persistence are attributable. The temporal reading of that semantical framework, laid out in §4, allows for the representation of all three major positions in the persistence debate: endurantism, perdurantism, and exdurantism. We claim that this supports the view that endurantism, our commonsensical theory of persistence, wins the day: there is no need for revision, as any purported advantages of the revisionistic positions of perdurantism and exdurantism come to nothing, given the semantical equivalence that we have shown.

Commonsensical endurantist persistence ain't broke. There is no need to fix it.

Acknowledgements

I thank Nuel Belnap for numerous illuminating and helpful discussions about the framework of case-intensional semantics and for his insightful comments on a previous version of this paper. Thanks to my audience at Bonn for a stimulating discussion, and to the referees for helpful comments. Support by VIDI grant 276-20-013 of the Netherlands Organization for Scientific Research is gratefully acknowledged.

Notes

1 As one referee remarked, "can" has a variety of uses. In the example, "This glass can be destroyed today", it is used in the sense of circumstantial modality as one form of root modality (see Kratzer, 1991). In contrast to the sentential operator form "It is possible that this glass is destroyed today", which normally has an epistemic reading ("It is compatible with all I know that ..."), circumstantial "can" modality has metaphysical import: it is modality in our world, based on real potentialities of things. See also Vetter (2010).

2 To some it will also seem quite dubious – apart from the worry mentioned in note 1, there is of course also a significant debate about the status and the right analysis of *de re* modality. See § 3.6 below for some comments.

3 As we will see, it will be enough for us if it is acknowledged that indeterminism is a (metaphysical) possibility: that already provides enough motivation to adopt a framework in which persistence can be represented in a novel, elucidating way.

4 This phrase is Lewis's, who attacks endurantism (Lewis, 1986, 202); it did not come up as an attempt at a useful positive characterization of endurantism. (See McCall and Lowe (2009) for relevant critique of Lewis's framing of the debate, as well as for the following positive characterization of endurance: "An object *endures* iff (i) it lacks temporal parts, and (ii) it exists at more than one time.") Still, the Lewisian phrase has stuck, so we will use it as well. It is however in need of elucidation. We aim at providing such elucidation below.

5 Never mind the fact that things can lose parts – e.g., shed a hair – and still remain the same. See note 4 above for the artificiality of the slogan.

6 We wish to remain neutral and not take a stance here as to whether there are implications between an A- or B-theory of time and the different views of persistence.

7 An A-theoretic reformulation may well be possible along the lines of Prior's idea of capturing B-theoretic model theory in A-theoretic terms; cf. his notion of "grades of tense-logical involvement" (Prior, 1968) and the ensuing development of hybrid logic, for which see, e.g., Blackburn (2000) and Braüner (2011).

8 At this stage, the *epistemic* possibility of a difference in extension is enough to motivate the assumption of a difference in intension (broadly

construed). In the framework of case-intensional semantics to be laid out below, it would depend on the details of the model under consideration whether the (technically specified) intensions of the mentioned predicates really differ or not.

9 Frege's notions of *Sinn* vs. *Bedeutung* do not coincide with the present-day distinction of intension vs. extension. Historically, however, they formed an important source of inspiration for the development of that distinction.

10 For a nice exposition of the framework, see Belnap (2006); for further developments, see Belnap and Müller (2012). We follow the latter in matters of detail.

11 Technically it turns out not to matter whether there is a single domain containing extensions at all cases, or there are different domains D_γ at different cases, as long as their cardinality is the same.

12 This does not limit expressivity, since necessary identity, i.e., identity in all cases, can be expressed as $\Box\alpha = \beta$, using the modal operator "necessarily" (or, idiomatically, "in any case") that quantifies over all cases; see § 3.4.

13 Hereby we certainly cannot give a reductive analysis of possibility: we have to know that the *cases* are possible before we can employ them here. The same holds true, however, of the more common possible worlds talk – actually, even more so in that mostly, over and above the *possible worlds*, a relation of *relative possibility* ("accessibility") is invoked.

14 More properly, relating to what was said about the extension and intension of predicates above, we say that the extension $ext_\gamma(E)$ of the existence predicate in a case γ consists of all those individual intensions $\mathfrak{I}$ (all functions $\mathfrak{I}$ from Γ to D) for which $\mathfrak{I}(\gamma) \neq N$. It turns out, as it should, that if we have $E\alpha \,\&\, \alpha = \beta$ in a case γ, then we also have $E\beta$ in that case.

15 In fact, in an Ockhamist theory such as case-intensional branching time, which is addressed briefly in note 23 below, there is no "real case", as none of the possible futures of an utterance context is singled out above all others. Bressan (1972) also motivates his general framework by examples from theoretical physics in which one cannot distinguish a "real case".

16 There is one relevant difference: "Socrates" refers to a human being, something falling under a sortal concept: a proper thing. "Socrates" is, in the terminology of Geach (1980), a *name for* a man. "The present king of France", on the other hand, picks out different human beings at different times; its individual intension therefore doesn't fall under any natural sort. See the discussion in § 3.8 below.

17 This meshes well with the fact that all open formulae create a potentially intensional context: even the atomic open formula Fx, for F an intensional predicate, is intensional.

18 It is well known that artefacts such as tables or cups pose specific challenges for the notion of persistence, as illustrated, for example, by Hobbes's famous example of Theseus's ship (see Wiggins, 2001, 93 f.). At the level of abstraction of the present paper, we will not be concerned with the specific question of artefact persistence, but just presuppose that the semantics gives us a way of singling out proper things as belonging to sorts. This semantic mechanism may well be context-dependent.

19 We are of course not after any specific thesis that the historical Aristotle held. It is a fact, however, that the label "Aristotelianism", or "neo-Aristotelianism", for a view of things as belonging to sorts has wide currency.
20 Case-intensional semantics easily provides the necessary higher-order machinery. For details, see Bressan (1972) or, more compactly, Belnap (2006) and Belnap and Müller (2012).
21 In this specific sense we may say that transsubstantiation, which has been a matter of life and death in the history of Christianity, is indeed, but luckily more theoretically, a matter of life and death.
22 We do not wish to take a stance on this issue; here it is enough to point out that the logical framework leaves this open as a metaphysical question, by being able to represent both options. Case- intensional logic is not metaphysics-driven logic, but meant to be a tool for clarifying metaphysical questions by providing adequate formal representations of differing views.
23 See Belnap and Müller (2012) for details. The branching time framework, based on ideas by Kripke (see Ploug and Øhrstrøm, 2011), Prior (1967b), and Thomason (1970), is described in detail in Belnap et al. (2001). It is important, in combining time and modality, to allow for incompatible cases at the same (clock-)time, so the cases shouldn't be called "times", but "moments". Ockhamist semantics for the future tense further complicates matters. For branching space-times, see Belnap (1992) and Müller (2010).

References

Belnap, Nuel, 1992: Branching space-time. *Synthese* 92(3), pp. 385–434.

Belnap, Nuel, 2006: Bressan's type-theoretical combination of quantification and modality. In: Lagerlund, H., Lindström, S., and Sliwinski, R. (eds.): *Modality Matters. Twenty-five Essays in Honor of Krister Segerberg*. Department of Philosophy, Uppsala University, pp. 31–53.

Belnap, Nuel, and Müller, Thomas, 2012: Case-intensional first order logic (I). Towards a logic of sorts. Forthcoming.

Belnap, Nuel, Perloff, Michael, and Xu, Ming, 2001: *Facing the future. Agents and choices in our indeterminist world*. Oxford: Oxford University Press.

Blackburn, Patrick, 2000: Representation, reasoning, and relational structures: a hybrid logic manifesto. In: *Logic Journal of IGPL*, 8(3), pp. 339–365.

Braüner, Torben, 2011: *Hybrid logic and its proof-theory*. Volume 37 of *Applied Logic Series*. Berlin: Springer.

Bressan, Aldo, 1972: *A general interpreted modal calculus*. New Haven, CT: Yale University Press.

Carnap, Rudolf, 1947: *Meaning and necessity: A study in semantics and modal logic*. Chicago: University of Chicago Press. (References are to 2nd ed., 1956).

Davidson, Donald, 1987: Knowing one's own mind. In: *Proceedings and Addresses of the American Philosophical Association* 60, pp. 441–458.

Geach, Peter T., 1980: *Reference and generality*. Ithaca, NY: Cornell University Press, 3rd edition. (1st edition, 1962).

Kratzer, Angelika, 1991: Modality. In: von Stechow, A. and Wunderlich, D. (eds.): *Semantics: An international handbook of contemporary research*. Berlin: de Gruyter, pp. 639–650.

Kripke, Saul, 1980: *Naming and necessity*. Oxford: Blackwell. (Originally published 1972).

Lewis, David K., 1986: *On the plurality of worlds*. Oxford: Blackwell.

Lowe, E. Jonathan, 2009: *More kinds of being*. Oxford: Blackwell.

McCall, Storrs, and Lowe, E. Jonathan, 2009: The definition of endurance. In: *Analysis* 69(2), pp. 277–280.

Meyer, Ulrich, 2005: The presentist's dilemma. In: *Philosophical Studies* 122, pp. 213–225.

Müller, Thomas, 2007: Prior's tense-logical universalism. In: *Logique et Analyse* 199, pp. 223–252.

Müller, Thomas, 2010: Towards a theory of limited indeterminism in branching space-times. In: *Journal of Philosophical Logic* 39, pp. 395–423.

Ploug, Thomas, and Øhrstrøm, Peter, 2011: Branching time, indeterminism and tense logic. Unveiling the Prior-Kripke letters. In: *Synthese*, DOI 10.1007/S11229-011-9944-2.

Prior, Arthur N., 1967a: Logic, modal. In: Edwards, P. (ed.): *Encyclopedia of philosophy, Vol. 5*. New York: Macmillan, p. 10.

Prior, Arthur N., 1967b: *Past, present and future*. Oxford: Oxford University Press.

Prior, Arthur N., 1968: *Papers on time and tense*, chapter XI: Tense logic and the logic of earlier and later, Oxford: Oxford University Press, pp. 116–134.

Russell, Bertrand, 1905: On denoting. In: *Mind* 14(56), pp. 479–493.

Savitt, Steven F., 2006: Presentism and eternalism in perspective. In: Dieks, D. (ed.): *The Ontology of Spacetime*. Amsterdam: Elsevier, pp. 111–127.

Sider, Ted, 1996: All the world's a stage. In: *Australasian Journal of Philosophy* 74, pp. 433–453.
Sider, Ted, 2001: *Four-dimensionalism. An Ontology of Persistence and Time*. Oxford: Oxford University Press.
Thomason, Richmond H., 1970: Indeterminist time and truth-value gaps. In: *Theoria*, 36, pp. 264–281.
Thompson, Michael, 2003: What is it to wrong someone? A puzzle about justice. In: Wallace, R. J., Pettit, P., Scheffler, S., and Smith, M (eds.): *Reason and value: Themes from the moral philosophy of Joseph Raz*. Oxford: Oxford University Press, pp. 333–384.
Vetter, Barbara, 2010: *Potentiality and possibility*. PhD thesis, Oxford University.
Wiggins, David, 2001: *Sameness and substance renewed*. Cambridge: Cambridge University Press.

Thorben Petersen

Explicating Eternalism – A Study in Metaontology

Abstract

The doctrine of eternalism is explicated. Since it is introduced as the denial of passagism (the doctrine that time objectively passes), it is also shown that the debate between eternalists and passagists amounts to a substantial ontological debate. The general strategy is to posit a distinction between a neutral kind of being in addition to various determined kinds of being. It is demonstrated that ontologists manage to set out and defend their respective ontological schemes in spite of disagreement by having mastered a corresponding schematic construction central to the language they use. Thus, although the eternalist understands what the passagist is trying to get at, he is able to reject existence of the supposed kind.

Zusammenfassung

Expliziert wird die ontologische Position des Äternalismus. Insofern diese als Verneinung des Passagismus eingeführt wird (also als Verneinung der These, daß Zeit objektiv vergeht), wird zugleich dargelegt, daß die Debatte zwischen Äternalisten und Passagisten eine substantielle ontologische Debatte darstellt. Motiviert wird diese durch eine grundlegende Unterscheidung zwischen einer neutralen Seinsweise gegenüber diversen determinierten Weisen, zu sein. Da sie über den korrespondierenden Begriff neutraler Existenz verfügen, sind Ontologen in der Lage, sich trotz divergierender Ansichten über ihre Entwürfe zu verständigen. Äternalisten können die Position der Passagisten dementsprechend nachvollziehen, ohne deren Ansicht zu teilen.

The aim of this paper is to explicate *eternalism* – the ontological doctrine, roughly, that there are no transient entities at the fundamental level of being. Over the course of doing so I shall likewise motivate the objective that the debate between eternalists and adherents of temporal becoming amounts to a substantial ontological debate. The proposal I am about to offer has these issues most intimately related to one another, which is basically because eternalism – very roughly – will be taken to be the denial of *passagism*. Since I shall mainly be concerned with establishing that there is something eternalists and passagists disagree *about*, what is to follow may well be considered as contributing to the flourishing industry of metaontology.

Perhaps I should indicate in advance that usually the debate is explicated as holding between eternalists and presentists. As will turn out in the course of this paper, a *passagist* in my sense is someone who objects – in some way or other – to the eternalist ontology. Thus passagists in my sense do include presentists, but growing and shrinking blockers, so-called maximal presentists and exotics such as converse presentists as well. Although for reasons metaphysical I take it that presentism is the only sustainable alternative to eternalism, I sense something common to all passagist ontologies. In a way, this allying common element just is what the eternalist ontology lacks, namely *transience*, i.e. *temporal passage* alias *becoming* or, as I shall call it throughout this paper, *the inclusion of temporal entities*. Accordingly, a temporal entity in my sense roughly is a transient entity, i.e. an entity that comes into being, enjoys existence for a while and then, finally, passes out of existence. Note, then, that I do not take eternalism to deny the existence of entities located in space and time or space-time or the existence of entities ordered by what McTaggart (1908) came to call a *B-series*. The doctrine merely objects to the idea that – in addition to or instead of being located in space and time or space-time (or forming a B-series etc.) – concrete entities also exhibit the characteristics of transience, i.e. the Whoosh and Whiz unreflected appearance suggests them to have.

In brief, my strategy is to posit a distinction between different determined kinds of being on the one hand and an additional entirely neutral way of being on the other. The general idea is to say that eternalists and passagists are agreed that the category of temporal entities *possibly* is one of the determined ways of being. I also argue that ontologists have established a certain language O in which they set out and defend their respective ontological schemes. Most crucially I take it that O features a highly schematic construction, namely [ϕs $\text{exist}_{\text{simp}}$], whose purpose is essentially twofold: First, instances of [ϕs $\text{exist}_{\text{simp}}$] can be used to make ontologically serious assertions (say 'spatiotemporal entities $\text{exist}_{\text{simp}}$'). Second, the construction enables competent speakers of O to recognize (certain) claims of opposed ontological schools as instances of existential claims. This enables me to define the doctrine of passagism as a certain instance of [ϕs $exist_{simp}$], namely the claim that *temporal* entities $exist_{simp}$, which eternalists are able to understand as well but reject. Thus on my view passagists not merely recognize the category of temporal entities to be *possibly* among the determined ways of being, but additionally hold that this category *actually is* one of these. This finally allows me to introduce eternalism as the denial of passagism, namely as the thesis that, actually, the category of temporal entities is not among the determined ways of being.

I. Prelude: The Sceptical Challenge

Let us begin by distinguishing the recently evolved metaontological[1] debate from the "mere" ontological debate between eternalists and passagists. Back in the good old days (roughly: up until the end of the 1990s[2]), there only was the eternalist school denying that there is such thing as temporal becoming and, secondly, the various faculties of the passagist school, each displaying firm belief in temporal becoming. The sceptic's appearance – presumably motivated by the seemingly endlessly continuing exchange of arguments – then effectively made for a second debate, the issue of which is to settle whether at all there is something for eternalists and passagists to disagree about. In a nutshell, the sceptic's provocative claim is that there is not: for some or other reason disagreement between self-styled eternalists and self-styled passagists is entirely pointless. Thus Callender (forthcoming) summarizes his review of the debate by saying that "… for all I have said, eternalism might just *be* presentism or possibilism in a different vocabulary." If Callender is right, of course, then we have no debate. Eternalists and passagists would at best be talking past each other. Further objections to the debate include the charge of triviality (at least one of the contesters spreads platitudes) and even inconsistency (some of the temporal ontologies' basic doctrines harbour contradictions). By my lights, however, the sceptical line of reasoning follows a certain logic that one should *not* comply with. In order to keep matter simple – the main goal of this paper is to explicate eternalism rather than scepticism concerning temporal ontology – I shall say that the underlying assumption here is that temporal ontologies are to be explicated in single isolated statements. The strategy then applied is to analyse these statements truth-theoretically, the focus being placed on what I shall call *temporally indexical constructions*.[3] Along this way the sceptic indeed succeeds in distilling some truisms and contradictions from what really ought to be grand metaphysical systems. A paradigm example is provided by the sceptic's take on Hilary Putnam's 1967 paper *Time and Physical Geometry*, which mobilizes special relativity theory in favour of eternalism. The crucial thing to note is that, strictly speaking, Putnam does not conclude that eternalism holds, but that "future things (or events) are already real" (cf. Putnam, 1967, 242). Granting that Putnam indeed chooses an unfortunate way of expressing his eleatic conclusion, I nevertheless take it to be obvious what he *intends* to say. His critics, however, do not mind weighing Putnam's words (see, for instance, Savitt, 2006; Dolev, 2007; and Dorato, 2008). In particular it is observed that the crucial phrase

(PUT) Future things are already real

features some constructions that are temporally indexical (namely present-tense plus temporal adverbials), thus prompting interpretation along one of the following lines:

(PUT_I) Future things are already real now.

(PUT_{II}) There will be future things.

Insofar (PUT_I) postulates coexistence in the sense of coexisting simultaneously, the sceptic reasons, eternalists and presentists will be happy to reject it alike, and we grant to the sceptic that indeed it is unwise to reject spatiotemporal variation *tout court*.[4] Unfortunately, the remaining interpretation is anything but a challenge. Stressing that presentists will subscribe to (PUT_{II}) as well, the sceptic concludes that eternalism and presentism are metaphysically equivalent at best. My second example is the so-called *presentist's dilemma*, which is likewise built upon the observation that basic tenets of the presentist manifesto, such as (F), i.e.

(F) Future things do not exist,

are inherently tensed. In particular, the construction 'exist' is said to be ambiguous between two interpretations, the first *seriously tensed*, the second *tenseless*:

(F_I) Future things do not exist now.
(F_{II}) Future things did not exist, do not exist and will not exist.

The intended conclusion, then, is that interpretation (F_I) is entirely trivial, while (F_{II}) harbours a contradiction. Somewhat more particularly, the presentist supposedly is forced to declare his worldview to be caught between the Scylla of a triviality and the Charybdis of a contradiction (cf. Dorato, 2008, 66).

I won't offer any further examples here and simply take it for granted instead that the hallmark of temporal-ontology scepticism is to follow the logic just described. However that be, the logic of the sceptical challenge is only of minor importance for our purposes. This is because this paper simply does not come in answering to the sceptic. Rather, the strategy employed is to show that there is a debate, which is why the sceptic *must* be wrong. I make a start by outlining some general metaontological principles and conditions that need to be met in order for two ontological schools *A* and *B* being in substantial disagreement (chapter II). In a second step I am going to apply these general principles, conditions and distinctions to temporal ontology (chapter III). I then shall introduce, discuss and finally reject some possible objections to my proposal (chapter IV).

II. Metaontology

What must be given in order to guarantee that two ontological schools *A* and *B* disagree substantially? My suggestion is that there are two conditions on this, namely

(i) there being a distinction between *neutral* and *determined existence &*
(ii) establishment of a certain language O, capable of implementing and delivering ontological disagreement.

O, of course, is the notorious *language of the ontology room*, sometimes alternately called *Ontologese.*[5] As regards the distinction between neutral and determined existence, we may alternately speak of the distinction between *plain existence* (or *existence simpliciter*) and *different kinds* (or *different ways*) *of being.* I shall say what this distinction is all about after having introduced (my version of) the language of the ontology room.

§ 1) The Language of the Ontology Room

As I just specified, no language can become the language of the ontology room unless it is capable of implementing and delivering ontological disagreement. Actually there are three requirements on a language's importing the presence of ontological disagreement, two of which govern concurrent usage of symbols.

In order to ensure that *A* and *B* speak the very same language first of all we demand *sameness of predicates* (α). For instance, in case that *B* denies *A*'s assertion that Sherry is his mate (trying a new example here), it seems as if *A* and *B* substantially disagree about Sherry's social status. But it is clear that this impression vanishes upon realizing that *A* is talking American English, while *B*'s tongue is British. Second we demand *sameness of ontologically serious constructions* (β). For again it is clear that *A* and *B* need not disagree in case that *B* denies *A*'s assertion 'There's a cup on the table' in case that *A* is geared to ordinary English, whereas *B* has made a try at talking some nihilistic slang of Ontologese, part of whose grammar is that the existential quantifier does not range over compound entities (be they gerrymandered or spatiotemporally continuous). Actually it is perfectly conceivable that – since *A* and *B* are merely talking past each other – they finally reach agreement. However, in case that *A* holds that compound entities exist with *B* emphatically denying employing the very same concept of existence, it rather seems that *B* is simply not willing to acknowledge one of the categories turning up on *A*'s ontological scheme. But this is just a roundabout way of saying that *A* and *B* are engaged in some substantial ontological disagreement. The third and final condition on O signalizing the presence of ontological *disagreement* is that what is symbolized (via using some appropriate construction C of O)[6] is capable both of being affirmed *and* negated (γ). For what does disagreement consist in if not two people showing different attitudes towards *one and the same* subject matter? Well, perhaps two sides showing *opposed* attitudes towards that issue, such that one person affirms what is at stake whereas the other denies it. Clearly, however, in order to allow opponents to show contrasting attitudes, the bone of contention must be capable of being affirmed and negated as well. Having thus characterized the language of the ontology room, we now turn to the distinction between neutral and determined existence.

§ 2) Neutral and Determined Existence

Now, what I am ultimately after as regards the distinction between neutral and determined existence is to make plausible a certain principle governing (the planning of) ontological schemata. This principle, call it (POS_1), demands that

(POS_1) No thing exists in some way without just plain existing.

If the principle holds, then in case that something exists qua being ϕ, (POS_1) *guarantees* that this certain something exists simpliciter ('$exists_{simp}$', for short) as well. Here 'ϕ' functions as a placeholder for designations of (certain) ontological categories, a systematic unity of which I take to constitute an *ontological scheme* or, alternately, a particular *ontology*. Prime examples for an ontological category ϕ include the category of spatiotemporal entities, the category of persisting entities and the category of abstract entities. Now, with respect to the planning of ontological schemata, (POS_1) demands something very reasonable from the ontologist. For illustrative purposes, consider ϕ to be the category of spatiotemporal entities. In case that ontologist NN holds that there are spatiotemporal entities, (POS_1) obliges NN to announce (as well) that spatiotemporal entities $exist_{simp}$. And that is substantially all there is to say about principle (POS_1). Formalization admittedly faces problems having to do with the notion of individuality, which is why I prefer to illustrate and motivate (POS_1) by way of example here. In particular, I show that in practice ontologists rely on (POS_1) or at least on a principle very much like it. The crucial point about (POS_1) anyway is that it highlights the notions of neutral and determined existence in some particular manner, the distinction of which can be independently motivated by way of example as well. I take (POS_1) to be accompanied by a sister-principle, which is (POS_2) and says that:

(POS_2) No thing $exists_{simp}$ without existing in some way.

This sister-principle may roughly be described as my version of Quine's famous slogan "No entity without identity" (cf. Quine, 1969, 23). However, when I say that entities exist in some way, I take it to mean that these entities are sorted by (different) category ϕ, i. e. sorted by (different) category in the sense advanced in this paper. I have nothing to say in defence of (POS_2) for now, except that I take it to be intuitively plausible. Assuming ontological realism, rejecting (POS_2) either amounts to saying that reality is some sort of amorphous lump or else some unsystematic collection of shoes and ships and sealing wax, of cabbages and kings.[7] Neither option is very promising, for reasons I cannot go into here, however. Let it finally be mentioned, then, that the impact of principles (POS_1) and (POS_2) obviously depends on what exactly I take ontological categories to be. Unfortunately, that is another issue to be dealt with another time. Suffice it to say that I am decidedly traditional in taking categories to be the most general kinds of things plausibly forming a hierarchical (and non-overlapping) unity, i.e. an ontological scheme or ontology.[8] In particular, I hold that some candidates are too specific to qualify as categories proper ('garment', 'chemical compound' or 'admirer of Sherry'). I also take it that in case the ontology is hierarchically ordered, at least some things "belong" to more than one category – for example, if something qualifies as enduring entity, it plausibly qualifies as persisting and spatiotemporal entity as well.[9] I have nothing to say about the status of categories themselves here, though it should be clear that I take them to be as mind-independent as can be.[10] Finally note that I do not take categories to be exemplifiable. This is because on my view exemplification is a relation solely pertaining to universals (and their instances), universals themselves being a *candidate* for an ontological category among others. What *exactly* the relation between categories and its "members" amounts to is a tricky issue I won't settle here. If needed, I will express myself saying that something "belongs" to category ϕ, while leaving the nature of that relation unspecified.

It is now time to motivate the distinction between neutral and determined existence. To this end, consider the case of holes. Holes, I take it, are – in some sense – ontologically dependent upon their hosts. Of course one could as well be inclined to reject their existence altogether, but authors with serious Ockhamist inclinations towards holes not merely face the formidable task of providing a translation scheme for ordinary hole-talk (into talk about perforated objects say; see Lewis and Lewis, 1970; and Turner, 2011). The perforational nihilist additionally owes us an explanation as to why it is that we have to measure the size of a hole in the same way that we measure anything real (cf. Azzouni, 2010, 15). For these and similar reasons it might be more reasonable to acknowledge that holes at least *in some sense* exist, i.e. that holes – despite their shadowy appearance – enjoy some *kind* of being. Thus Karmo (1977) takes holes to be *disturbances*. In a similar vein the threesome Wake, Spencer and Fowler (2007) conceives of holes as *regions of spacetime*, while McDaniel (2010) speaks of *almost nothings* (the operative word clearly being 'almost' here). The particular details of these proposals need not concern us here. What matters is that any attempt at categorization testifies to the general distinction between determined and plain existence. The crucial thing to note is that once we grant to holes some categorical status, the status of disturbances say, we are *eo ipso* committed to say that there is a way in which holes and their hosts exist *alike*. This is because to say that holes exist *qua disturbances* analytically implies that holes exist *simpliciter*. In other words, then, one cannot understand what it is for something to be in some way without conceiving of it as existing.[11] What is most significant about this line of reasoning is that it in no way hinges on the particular example chosen. Thus in case that holes indeed turn out to be reducible to (or, rather, eliminable in favour of) some more basic sort of entity (such as the hole-linings of the Lewises), of course they not remotely contribute to the distinction between determined and plain existence, for in that case holes do not exist at all. There are plenty of other cases to the rescue, however, and I discuss these in much more detail in my Petersen (in preparation).[12]

But what is so crucial about recognising this neutral way of being? To start with, it should be clear that I take the *concept* of existence simpliciter to be among the ontologically serious constructions of *O*. The main point about this particular concept is that it enables us to become *selective* about ontological categories. More particularly, distinguishing between determined existence and existence simpliciter allows ontologists to *articulate* their selectivity about *certain* ontological categories *comprehensibly*. Accordingly, this variety of existence pluralism breeds mutual understanding insofar it allows for recognizing each other's ontological ambitions, while disagreeing, and substantially so, about what exists – and how. Thus in distinguishing between determined and plain existence speakers of *O* establish a schematic construction [ϕs $\text{exist}_{\text{simp}}$] enabling them to recognize (certain) claims of opposed ontological schools as instances of existential claims. This granted the second point to stress is that disagreement about what exists is rather common practice among ontologists, and actually there is not much reason to suspect that this common practice could be altogether pointless. On the contrary, rather, being regularly used, *O* is intact and thriving, thus indicating that indeed there is something *about* this language. Nihilists, for example, deny *compound* existence, i.e. existence of compound entities, although they clearly have an idea of what compound entities would be like – if only they existed$_{simp}$. As far as I am concerned, there is no reason to doubt that nihilists understand what kind of existence they reject. In fact it seems much more plausible to assume that their disapproval is partially due to their grasping what reality would be like if compound entities existed$_{simp}$. The general thesis, accordingly, is that each of these schools is (partially) motivated to reject the kind of existence it does because of having an adequate idea of what reality would be like in case that entities of the supposed kind existed$_{simp}$. By implementing the abovementioned highly schematic construction [ϕs exist$_{simp}$] we may roughly define substantial ontological disagreement as follows:

(SOD) Schools *A* and *B* substantially disagree about ontological category ϕ iff there is a proposition p such that (i) *A* affirms p and (ii) *B* denies p and (iii) p is an instance of the form [ϕs exist$_{simp}$].

For example, in line with (SOD), platonists and nominalists are in substantial disagreement insofar platonists affirm that abstract entities exist$_{simp}$, while nominalists deny precisely *this*, i.e. that abstract entities exist$_{simp}$. Armed with this distinction it is now time to turn to temporal ontology.

III. Temporal Ontology

The question we need to address is: Which instance of [ϕs exist$_{simp}$] need eternalists and passagists disagree about in order for their debate to be substantial? The answer that I shall defend in this paper is that passagists should say that (T_{EC}), i.e.:

(T_{EC}) Temporal entities exist$_{simp}$,

while eternalists should deny precisely *this*, i.e. that temporal entities exist$_{simp}$. Now, in line with condition (α) (the *sameness-of-predicates condition*), my proposal has it that there cannot be disagreement on this matter unless eternalists and passagists agree on the meaning of 'temporal' in (T_{EC}). In the previous section it was argued that O features highly schematic construction [ϕs exist$_{simp}$] enabling ontologists to recognize each other's ontological ambitions in spite of disagreement. Thus eternalists and passagists should be able to meet condition (β) (i.e. *sameness of ontologically serious constructions*). Obviously, however, in order to disagree on the *same* subject matter (the demand of which is also tacit in (γ)), eternalists and passagists furthermore need to agree what the inclusion of temporal entities amounts to (i.e. what the world would be like in case that temporal entities $\text{existed}_{\text{simp}}$). How then to characterize temporal entities? Actually this task is less complicated than it first may appear, for all it principally takes is some rough and ready description. Of course, given that (β) is met, the sceptic cannot accept that 'temporal' allows for illustration. But then he should realize that my categorical proposal paves the way for a different perspective – a perspective, that is, from which a rather simple explication suffices. The only constraint on possible candidate meanings of 'temporal' I can think of is that eternalists and passagists need to recognize these as such. In other words, the characterization we finally come up with must figure in the actual debate between passagists and eternalists. I take it, then, that my proposal can do with saying that temporal entities are simply those entities that come into being and pass (or fade) away. Somewhat less poetically we may say that temporal entities are those entities that begin and cease to exist. Passagists argue that entities of this kind $\text{exist}_{\text{simp}}$, whereas eternalists deny that they do. And this is what they differ about.

Some comments are in order, though. First, the categorical proposal at hand obviously does away with attributing a special status to *time*, i.e. a status distinguishing passage from other ontological categories.[13] In a way this is just what my proposal is all about – conceiving of temporal entities in terms of ontological category in order to achieve conformation to other phenomena. This demotion naturally carries over to the planning of ontological schemes, so that the question about time does not become a question to be answered over and above any questions concerning in- or exclusion of the remaining categories.[14] On the current proposal doing ontology starts by acknowledging that at least something $\text{exists}_{\text{simp}}$, and it is only in a second step that bare existence becomes furnished, so to speak. For illustrative purposes, consider ontological scheme Ω, which recognizes *spatiotemporal* and *abstract* existence, say. Thus according to Ω, spatiotemporal and abstract entities $\text{exist}_{\text{simp}}$. Furthermore suppose that some of its proponents (the omegists) feel the need to augment Ω (perhaps careful study convinced these renegade omegists that their ontology is much too slim to meet some of philosophy's most intriguing questions). Now, perhaps augmented ontology Ω^+ additionally recognizes Cartesian existence (the existence of Cartesian souls, that is), while managing to do without mere possible existence, but for now the important question to ask, of course, is whether Ω^+ recognizes *temporal* existence. More precisely, then, the important question to ask is whether Ω^+ recognizes temporal existence *in addition to* or spatiotemporal and abstract existence (or, rather, in addition to abstract and *instead of* spatiotemporal existence). And by now it should be clear that the passagist will answer this question affirmatively, whereas the eternalist – to speak with Wittgenstein here – will leave everything as it is.

The second thing to say is that on the current proposal it is the passagist's burden to make *his* an attractive point of view. Basically this is because the inclusion of temporal entities would come as an addition to being_{simp}, which obviously makes it a move in need of justification. In other words, being an addition to bare existence, the inclusion of temporal entities is something that needs to be argued for. This is not to say that the category of time is somehow different from other categories, for according to the current proposal the inclusion of every determined way of being counts as an addition to being_{simp}. On closer consideration, then, we rather shall say that the inclusion of any category whatsoever needs argument. For example, there are some excellent reasons to allow for spatiotemporal entities (entities located in spacetime, that is) and there are also some good reasons to allow for persisting entities as well. There even might be some reasons to allow for enduring entities. Are there also some reasons to allow for temporal entities? This is the question to be addressed by the passagist. By the same token the eternalist – although having an idea of what reality would be like in case that temporal entities existed_{simp} – may well be content with acknowledging spatiotemporal, persisting and even enduring entities, while wholeheartedly rejecting temporal entities. This concludes the outline of my proposal. Eternalism, I take it, comes down to rejecting the category of temporal entities. In what follows, I turn to some possible objections to my categorical proposal.

IV. Objections

As far as I can see, objections against my proposal fall in two broad camps, namely into those objections directed against the underlying metaontology which I am proposing and into those objections directed against the classification of time as an ontological category amongst others. As Thomas Müller has pointed out to me, one could also argue that often a real ontological debate gets its bite from claims of reduction. However, whether or not this be the case, this is certainly not an objection directed against my proposal. At most the suggestion could force me to explain what, precisely, it is that makes my proposal superior to the reductionist approach (indeed the two approaches might even naturally go together).

Let me introduce and discuss objections against the underlying metaontology first. Since I offer some thoroughgoing analysis of this issue in my Petersen (in preparation), I shall be very brief about it here. As far as I can see, there are principally two objections to the underlying metaontology I am proposing, namely an entirely general and, moreover, entirely thoroughgoing rejection of the idea that language somehow hooks up to the real world and, of course, the rejection of the distinction between neutral and determined existence, which I discuss first.

§ 1a) Rejecting the Neutral-Determined Distinction

This move may either take the form of rejecting (POS_1) or (POS_2) or both of these, neither option is very plausible, however. First, to reject both (POS_1) *and* (POS_2) is to wave ontological realism goodbye, which is tantamount to changing the subject. Second, rejecting (POS_2) is implausible for the reason already given in chapter II, which, to recall, is that the consequences of this move – taking reality to be some sort of amorphous lump or else some highly unstructured collection of shoes and ships and sealing wax etc. – do not seem to be very attractive. Third, rejecting (POS_1) is implausible for the reasons given in chapter II, i.e. *utterly* implausible since in practice ontologists actually distinguish between neutral and determined existence. This is why I take it that the metaontology proposed here gets things wrong just in case language does not catch up with the real world *at all*, which brings us to the second objection.

§ 1b) Rejecting the Language-World Fit
This second objection displays a rather hostile attitude, but I can vouch for some satisfaction with that, since it neither seems fair nor is it going to be plausible. The crucial thing to note is that I do not claim O to be a language from which the world's structure may simply be read off, which of course would be to claim something entirely implausible. However, nothing prevents us from distinguishing between *different degrees* of language-world fit – if I may say so – say from a total match over "some correspondence" to zero-fit. Given these different degrees of the language-world fit, we may happily grant that *some* conceptions on which the world "answers" to language are misguided indeed. Thus it seems rather shiftless to posit a fact, the constituents of which are Sherry and the particularized property of her smiling (plus some metaphysical glue, perhaps), that answers to the declarative sentence 'Sherry is smiling'. I likewise feel uneasy about inferring the existence of the category of events from sentences containing adverbial phrases such as 'Sherry changed her mind quickly'. Finally recall that a major part of this paper is devoted to the issue of convincing *you*, dear reader, that no conclusions about temporal ontology should be drawn from certain semantical features of language. These particular issues, however, are a far cry from the astonishing claim that language is not about the world *at all*. The important question to ask accordingly is whether O is in any sense presumptuous in imposing structure on the world.

Is O assuming too much structure on the world, then? The centrepiece of my proposal is that speakers of O have established a highly schematic ontologically serious construction, namely [ϕs $\text{exist}_{\text{simp}}$], instances of which can be used to make ontologically serious assertions. By the same token [ϕs $\text{exist}_{\text{simp}}$] enables speakers of O to recognize (certain) claims of opposed ontological schools as instances of existential claims. Thus the nominalist, let's say, does not believe a single word of what the platonist says. Clearly, however, he is able to *understand* what the platonist is trying to get at. In other words, the nominalist is able to sort of mimic what the world would be like in case that abstract entities $\text{exist}_{\text{simp}}$ and he is able to do so – partially at least – for having mastered highly schematic construction [ϕs $\text{exist}_{\text{simp}}$] – or something very similar to it. But this is nearly all there is to say about O. It is furthermore of considerable importance, though, that O is actually intact and thriving. The language of the ontology room is regularly (and increasingly) being spoken and unless one goes entirely pessimistic as regards the language-world fit, there is little reason to suspect that competent speakers of *O* are merely talking past each other. I take it, then, that *O* is indeed assuming some structure on the world, but certainly not too much. Actually, its core – as has just been shown – is rather undemanding. Accordingly, the metaontology proposed here gets things wrong just in case language does not catch up with the real world *at all*, which is utterly implausible.

Turn, then, to those objections directed against the classification of time as an ontological category amongst others. Again there are two objections I shall deal with, the first of which says that it is not legitimate to treat time on a par with other ontological categories, the second that we illegitimately ignore certain semantical properties of ontologically sensitive constructions.

§ 2a) Reality as essentially transient

The first objection I can think of is to say that it is not legitimate to treat time on a par with other ontological categories or, alternately, that it is illegitimate to separate transience from being$_{simp}$. This line of reasoning obviously rests on the assumption that being$_{simp}$ is essentially transient, whence the complaint that being is possibly a-transient or "static" (in case that eternalism holds, that is). I happily grant that there is something to this argument, namely that in case reality *is* essentially transient, my story about time as a determined mode of being gets things entirely wrong. However, the only person that may *sensibly* put forward this sort of complaint is the passagist, of course. This is because the argument's basic premise that reality is essentially temporal is – being an article of faith of the passagist ontology – deemed meaningless by the sceptic and thus cannot be used to rationalize the claim that transience should not be separated from being$_{simp}$. I therefore conclude that the first argument against my proposal badly misfires.

§ 2b) Shying away from semantics? The argument from indexicality

The second blow is built around the complaint that the proposal at hand illegitimately backs away from certain semantical – namely indexical – properties of ontologically serious constructions. More precisely, then, the objection is that we entirely leave out of consideration that ontologically serious constructions, such as 'exist$_{simp}$' in (T_{EC}), i. e.

(T_{EC}) Temporal entities exist_{simp},

are inherently (or else morphologically) tensed. Being tensed, these phrases are taken to be temporally indexical in the sense that on each use they inter alia reflect a different context of use or – put less sophisticated – a different time of speaking, which finds expression in the corresponding truth conditions. Now, although I happily grant that we have been careless of semantics so far, I fail to see how this should be worrisome. What, precisely, is it that is so bad about shying away from semantics? As was outlined in some more detail in the first chapter, the sceptic's answer is that explications of temporal ontologies come in isolated statements, which, in turn, can be analysed with regard to their literal truth-conditions. Thus Savitt (2006, 113) cites the following lines from Sider (1999, 326):

(Eternalism_{SID}) There *are* such things as merely past and merely future entities.

The crucial point is that Savitt explicitly notes that the verbal construction here is tensed, thus allowing for different interpretations of eternalism, every single one of which is taken to result in triviality or contradiction, however. To this I reply that the sceptic's strategy crucially involves a misleading description of the original debate. There is thus good reason to reject the logic of his conciliatory proposal. In what follows I shall outline where exactly his reasoning goes wrong.

Our target sentence, recall, is (T_{EC}). Now first of all concede that it is wholly beyond doubt that (T_{EC}) is inherently tensed (via 'exist_{simp}' that is). We may furthermore concede that, consequently, there is a sense in which different uses of (T_{EC}) *reflect* different contexts of use. This hardly makes for a problem, though. For whenever push comes to shove, passagists will subscribe to (T_{EC}) while eternalists will refrain from it – in fact the dispute couldn't be any more substantial. Moreover, it simply does not do here insisting that the contexts *tacitly* reflected in datable uses of (T_{EC}) exhibit certain characteristics pertaining to the realm of the temporal. It is quite plausible to consider any context *c* tacitly reflected in different uses *u* of (T_{EC}) to be (part of) the truthmaker of *u* as *interpreted literally*. However, a truthmaker thus considered is either transient or not. Somewhat more particularly, then, a truthmaker in this sense is transient in case that passagism holds and otherwise (i.e.

"static") in case that eternalism holds. Thus there is next-to-nothing for sceptics to draw from tacit reflection of context. To cause troubles the sceptic would at least have to hold that constructions which are ontologically serious and inherently tensed (such as 'exist$_{simp}$') express a special (passagist or presentist) quantifier (say 'there exist$_{simp}$ now'), ranging over nothing more than what is simultaneous with its use. Accordingly, utterances of (T_{EC}^{+}), i.e.

(T_{EC}^{+}) Temporal entities exist$_{simp}$ now,

would be true just in case temporal entities exist$_{simp}$ now, the truth-conditions specified here being obviously *homophonic.* This seems to be a case in which eternalists and passagists would indeed be speaking two different languages with their quantifiers carving up the world differently. However, this proposal runs afoul of my conception according to which opposed ontological schools have – in distinguishing between determined and plain existence – established highly schematic ontologically serious construction [ϕs exist$_{simp}$] enabling them to recognize each other's ontological ambitions in spite of disagreement. But let that pass for the moment. Even if we were to grant the sceptic that the passagist community uses a special quantifier, it is still quite hard to see the problem. This is because rejecting the homophonic treatment of (T_{EC}^{+}) suffices to reopen the debate and I can see no reason keeping eternalists from doing so. More precisely, if (T_{EC}^{+}) is true just in case temporal entities exist$_{simp}$ now (where 'exist$_{simp}$ now' is sensitive but to those things that are simultaneous with uses of (T_{EC}^{+})), then the obtaining of the eternalist ontology would render (T_{EC}^{+}) false. Full stop.

However, my major worry about the argument form indexicality is that this complaint builds on an unnecessarily strong variety of ultra-minimalist semantics.[15] As was demonstrated shortly, the logic of this sort of argument is to relate the truth-conditions of *what it said* in different uses of (T_{EC}) most intimately to the *literal* truth conditions of the corresponding sentence type. Accordingly, we should not really be surprised at the sceptic's ability to come up with a sense in which different uses of (T_{EC}) are made true (or else are rendered false) by different bits of the world, if I may say so. By my lights, however, this interpretation of (T_{EC}) is anything but self-suggesting. On the contrary, rather, I take it that whenever someone seriously utters (T_{EC}), he does not at all intend to say something about the present moment but *something dif-*

ferent instead. What I suggest, accordingly, is that we stress the *actual*, pragmatically enriched truth-conditions of (T_{EC}) instead of clinging to what it possibly might literally say. This in fact comprises two different issues, namely determining what one does not intend expressing using (T_{EC}) for one thing (i.e. carving out what (T_{EC}) literally says) and uncovering what actually one intends expressing for another. Now, this latter issue is in fact more demanding than the first (quite so), but for our purposes it will do to come up with a rough story here, which I shall outline in just a moment.

What one does not intend expressing using (T_{EC}), for that matter, should be clear by now. Namely one does not intend to say something about the present moment (such as that temporal entities $exist_{simp}$ right now). It has already been granted that indeed there is a sense in which different uses of (T_{EC}) are made true (or else rendered false) by different bits of the world. This is captured by the literal truth-conditions of (T_{EC}). Somewhat more particularly, then, according to the basic Kaplan-Perry account the (conventionalized) linguistic meaning of a certain temporally indexical construction C_{TI} is such that it (i) directs us from context of utterance c_u to referent or content, where, crucially, (ii) the linguistic meaning is not part of the content expressed with respect to *c*. The meaning of the temporal adverb 'now', for instance, roughly is *the moment at which this token is used*, its contribution to the proposition expressed with respect to a certain context c_u being nothing more (and nothing less) than the proposition's temporal element (roughly, a time), and a very similar story can be told about present-tense constructions such as 'smiles' and, arguably, 'exists' (or '$exists_{simp}$'). Thus on the Kaplan-Perry account the character of the temporally indexical construction '$exist_{simp}$' (as is featured in (T_{EC})) directs us from context of utterance c_u to referent or content, where the linguistic meaning is not part of the content expressed with respect to *c*. Instead its contribution to the proposition expressed with respect to context c_u is the proposition's temporal element. But whatever its temporal element may be *categorically speaking* – a state of affairs, say, or an event – that temporal element will be transient in case that passagism holds and otherwise (i.e. "static") in case that eternalism holds. Moreover – and this of course is the crucial thing to note here – the time of speaking is simply not what utterances of (T_{EC}) are primarily about. If at all time of speaking is triggered by linguistic rule plus context of utterance – according to the basic Kaplan-Perry account that is.[16] But surely that is just part of the semantics of (T_{EC}) and not of the pragmatics in play inside the ontology room. So what about the pragmatics, then? What is it that one intends to express in seriously asserting (T_{EC})? In light of what was said above, the following is a plausible story: If someone seriously asserts that temporal entities $exist_{simp}$, what he most plausibly means is that he recognizes the category of temporal entities. In other words again, if someone seriously asserts that temporal entities $exist_{simp}$, he most plausibly is an ontologist claiming that the category of temporal existence is part of his ontological scheme. And if someone denies that temporal entities $exist_{simp}$, he most plausibly is an ontologist claiming that the category of temporal existence is not part of his ontological scheme. I thus conclude that the argument from indexicality fails.

Here, then, is the expected reply: It will most likely be urged that we have failed to clarify what, precisely, temporal existence consists in. Although our objector may generously grant that it is fastidious to highlight the semantical properties of '$exist_{simp}$' in (T_{EC}), he will press hard for an explication of 'temporal existence'. For surely any explication of 'temporal existence' will be inherently (or else morphologically) tensed? In chapter III, temporal entities were introduced as those entities that *come into being and fade away*. Somewhat less metaphorically we might alternately say that temporal entities are those entities that *begin and cease to exist*. This, then, makes for the following paraphrase of (T_{EC}):

(T_{EC}*) Entities that begin and cease to exist $exist_{simp}$.

Allow me to first clarify the dialectic: As far as I can see, it is the passagist's duty to offer some reason to believe in (T_{EC}*), while the eternalist at most needs to show that there are reasons to believe (T_{EC}*) to be false. Passagists and eternalists are obviously allied, however, for being in need to prove (T_{EC}*) intelligible. The sceptic, by contrast, succeeds in case he is able to demonstrate (T_{EC}*) to be either unintelligible or trivial. So far, so good. Start, then, by granting that (T_{EC}*) indeed has a weird ring. Is it a grammatical sentence at all? How to interpret (the first occurrence of) 'exist'? And, moreover, what about it's being inherently tensed? However, by paraphrasing (T_{EC}*) appropriately, it turns out that *at least some* of these problems are spurious:

(T_{EC}**) There are_{simp} entities that begin and cease to exist.

Logically speaking, (T_{EC}**) is on a par with existential claims like 'There are$_{simp}$ entities that merely possibly exist' or 'There are$_{simp}$ entities that have abstract existence'. It thus can no longer be doubtful whether we are presented with a grammatical sentence. Doubts remain, however, concerning the interpretation of 'exist' (as occurring in the nominal phrase 'entities that begin and cease to exist'). Basically, the complaint is that there is danger of mingling temporal existence and existence$_{simp}$, in case of which we are robbed of our neutral way of existence. I happily grant that this indeed is a problem from the eternalist point of view. For if eternalists are robbed of their neutral way of existence this way (i.e. by mingling temporal existence and existence$_{simp}$), existence$_{simp}$ would be essentially temporal, which, of course, is the precise opposite of what the eternalist intends. It is absolutely crucial to note, however, that the resulting picture portrays the quintessence of passagism. Once more, then, this route is *not* open for the sceptic. Consequently, the sole remaining option for the sceptic is to read (T_{EC}**) as seriously tensed. Once more, however, this move does not appear to be a plausible move. For reading (T_{EC}**) seriously tensed either gives us (T_{EC}**$_{TS1}$) or (T_{EC}**$_{TS2}$), i.e.:

(T_{EC}**$_{TS1}$) There are$_{simp}$ now entities that begin and cease to exist.
(T_{EC}**$_{TS2}$) There are$_{simp}$ now$_1$ entities that now$_1$ begin and now$_1$ cease to exist now$_1$.

If we take (T_{EC}**$_{TS1}$) to be a meaningful sentence at all, I can see no reason why eternalists shouldn't deny it thus entering into a substantial debate with passagists. In any case, however, (T_{EC}**$_{TS1}$) and (T_{EC}**$_{TS2}$) do not amount to plausible interpretations of (T_{EC}**) at all. Although there might be a sense in which either (T_{EC}**$_{TS1}$) or (T_{EC}**$_{TS2}$) gives us what (T**) *literally* says, none of these paraphrases identifies what is *actually meant* by utterances of this sentence type. Thus I stick to my conviction that the argument from indexicality fails.

Conclusion

Ontology tries to answer the lasting question 'What is there?'. The metaontological enterprise is to figure out whether principally there are answers to the ontological question. Among the questions of ontology, finally, is the question whether there are temporal entities. In my view, the pre-theoretical answer to this question is a definite yes. Naïve answers presumably impart some impatience as well: *How could you ask such foolish question?* However, in brushing this question aside, the man on the street in no way reveals his sceptical tendencies. It is rather that untutored mind takes time to be *obviously* passing. When we come to learn, however, that certain metaphysical problems suggest the existence of a static universe and that fundamental physics might be altogether incompatible with objective passage, whereas phenomenological analysis reveals some sort of inner sense of time, we are no longer *sure* whether time indeed does pass. Thus reason suggests to us that the answer to the ontological question for temporal entities *could* be no. The sceptic, however, is unwilling to recognize this situation as posing a question. Finding it hard to understand *how* one could fail to see the problem here, I would like to think of the sceptic as taking a particular metaontological point of view.

In this paper I have argued that this particular metaontology is false. A cursory glance at ontological practice reveals that ontologists have established a certain language in which they set out and defend their respective ontologies. This language additionally enables competent speakers to recognize each other's ontological ambitions in spite of disagreement. I pointed out that the language of the ontology room is rather modest in assuming structure onto the world, such that its demands fail to be met just in case the language-world fit is a total zero. Now, from an ontological point of view, this is no great news, of course. For the consequence of this is that the debate between eternalists and passagists is to be settled by way of argument, which, of course, is just what participants of the original debate already thought. However, metaontologically something is gained, if even we know now that we may return to the original debate – without being afraid of making too much ado about nothing, that is.[17]

Notes

1 As is well known, there is, ironically, some dispute over how to distinguish ontology from metaphysics. Thus Ingarden (1964), for instance, takes metaphysics to deal with what is actual (and thus with categories fulfilled or occupied in my sense), ontology instead being concerned with

logical space. My usage of 'ontology' is rather based on the question 'What exists?', which is why I conceive of eternalists and passagists as being ontologists by profession. Accordingly I take this paper to be a study in metaontology instead of qualifying as a contribution to metametaphysics. Usually, however, metaphysicians are ontologists as well, and there will be occasions, in which for stylistic reasons I use 'ontology' and 'metaphysics' interchangeably.

2 Perhaps the first contribution to the substantiality debate is Williams (1996). Its present shape is more clearly discernable in Sider (1999, esp. 326/7) however.

3 From a purely *linguistic* point of view, the notion of a construction used here is that of Goldberg (2006). For a start I shall say that a construction *C* is temporally indexical just in case its associated rule of use plus context of utterance trigger potentially different primary contents. Textbook examples of temporally indexical constructions include inherent and morphological tense as well as temporal adverbs.

4 Here I would like to stress that I say 'spatiotemporal variation' instead of 'transition'. In my view, the concept of *transition* closely resembles the concept of *passage* – if it is cognitively different at all. But some authors, such as Williams (1996), have maintained that nothing is a theory of time unless it makes reference to some sort of transition, from which they finally conclude that there is no substantial difference between A-time and B-time (between eternalism and passagism, that is). Employing the concept of spatiotemporal *variation* here is meant to block this sort of reasoning in the first place. However, these misconceptions of B-time have already been pointed out long ago by Grünbaum (see Grünbaum (1967)).

5 See, for instance, Hirsch, 2008; Sider, 2009; and Korman, forthcoming. As is adumbrated in chapters (II, § 1) and (IV, § 1b) and worked out with attention to smaller details in my Petersen (in preparation), however, these author's understanding of Ontologese significantly differs from mine.

6 Here I take a construction C of O to be appropriate just in case it can be used without further ado to make an ontological assertion. Candidate constructions include 'There is/are', '... exists/exists$_{simp}$' (plus grammatical variations), as well as '... is real' (plus grammatical variations) and, arguably, '∃'.

7 Not forgetting dragons, witches, ectoplasm and the philosopher's stone as well as references to Lewis Carroll drawn from Lowe (2006, 7).

8 Here I draw from Westerhoff (2005).

9 As Westerhoff (2005, 19) points out, most ontological systems feature a *supercategory* at the highest level of the categorical hierarchy, which covers *everything* the ontology acknowledges. Westerhoff's supercategory closely resembles my additional neutral way of being insofar both comprise everything there is (according to the ontology in question). I hesitate, though, characterizing this as the highest or most fundamental category. For my purposes it entirely suffices to have an additional neutral category sensitive to all there is and that *could possibly* be "at the top" (or "fundamental").

10 Although not arguing the case here, I furthermore *tend* to favour necessitism with respect to categories, by which I mean that if something qualifies as ontological category at all, then it does so of (metaphysical) necessity. Here I would part ways with Westerhoff, who defends local *as well as* global relativism with respect to ontological categories (cf. Westerhoff, 2005, esp. 118ff.; and 207ff.).

11 To some extent this is just the opposite of the Meinongian principle that the *Sosein* of a *Gegenstand* is entirely independent of its *Sein* (cf. Mally, 1904, though clearly I am simply not willing here to distinguish between being (in the appropriate sense) and existence. Another conception incompatible to my own proposal, then, is *Noneism* (see, for instance, Priest, 2005).

12 Some authors, such as Steven Savitt, hold that they do not understand the concept of existence simpliciter (see, for instance, Savitt, 2006, 119ff.). To this I reply that the concept of existence simpliciter well might be inexplicable, but this is not to say that it is altogether impossible to come to an understanding or arrangement on what 'existence simpliciter' means. Roughly, my strategy to this end is to consider the attempt at categorization. I find it save to say that even deflationists should allow for difference in ways of being. Suppose, then, that the sceptic is willing to distinguish things of sort φ from things of sort ϕ, say spatiotemporal things from abstract entities. In order to illustrate to the sceptic what we mean by 'existence simpliciter', then, we could ask: "You doubt that the concept of existence simpliciter makes sense, fair enough. But besides the differences you discern between spatiotemporal and abstract entities, don't you recognize something common to them? Does it not occur to you at all that there's something they share?" And here I think it quite implausible to give a negative answer. Concluding the arrangement, we might add: "This common element is what 'existence simpliciter' is meant to capture."

13 This should not strike us as *too* big a surprise, however. In fact we already *knew* that time is not an all-embracing category: First of all, we lack clear intuitions concerning the case of time in mere possible worlds. Secondly, there is some discussion, originally initiated by McTaggart (1908), as regards the "fictional A-series". Third, there is ongoing controversy whether God is in time (cf. Helm, 2011). In any case, however, there is at least one category escaping temporality altogether, namely the category of abstract entities (where here I think of abstract entities in a strict sense, according to which mere possibilities and fictional entities do *not* qualify as abstract entities proper). As Cord Friebe has rightly pointed out to me, on ersatzist versions of presentism the existence of non-present times is secured by construing these as abstract entities, which hence do not escape temporality altogether. Unfortunately I cannot discuss this intriguing issue here, but for my part this consequence rather tells against ersatzist takes on presentism or, more generally, against any view that has abstract entities equipped with temporal elements.

14 In this vein, the schema presented in Lowe (2006), for instance, does not recognize any temporal category at all, indicating that time is taken to be somehow special.

15 My notion of *ultra-minimalist semantics* varies Recanati (2004).

16 I take it that the outcome is the same on any other account as well. These, of course, include the Bolzano-Frege view, the Russellian picture as well as the Lewisian conception.

17 I would like to give special thanks to my Bremen colleagues, in particular Meinard Kuhlmann, Paul Näger and Manfred Stöckler. I also would like to address my thanks to all the participants of the *Temporal Existence and Persistence in Spacetime* conference in Bonn, and here in particular to Yuri Balashov, Natalja Deng, Mauro Dorato, Florian Fischer, Cord Friebe, Cody Gilmore, Thomas Müller, Steven Savitt and Rainer Stuhlmann-Laeisz. Finally, I am grateful for receiving language corrections from Alexander Japp and Tim Hesse.

References

Azzouni, Jody, 2010: *Talking About Nothing. Numbers, Hallucinations and Fictions.* Oxford: Oxford University Press.

Callender, Craig, forthcoming: Time's Ontic Voltage. In: Bardon, Adrian (ed.): *Future of Philosophy of Time.* New York/London: Routledge.

Dolev, Yuval, 2007: *Time and Realism. Metaphysical and Antimetaphysical Perspectives.* Cambridge, MA: The MIT Press.

Dorato, Mauro, 2008: Putnam on Time and Special Relativity: A Long Journey from Ontology to Ethics. In: *European Journal Of Analytic Philosophy* 2 (4), pp. 51–73.

Goldberg, Adele, 2006: *Constructions at Work. The Nature of Generalization in Language.* Oxford: Oxford University Press.

Grünbaum, Adolf, 1967: The Status of Temporal Becoming. In: *Annals of the New York Academy of Sciences* 138, pp. 374–95.

Helm, Paul, 2011: *Eternal God. A Study of God without Time* (Second, Expanded Edition). Oxford: Oxford University Press.

Hirsch, Eli, 2008: Language, Ontology and Structure. In: *Nous* 3 (42), pp. 509–28.

Ingarden, Roman, 1964: *Der Streit um die Existenz der Welt.* Tübingen: Niemeyer.

Karmo, Toomas, 1977: Disturbances. In: *Analysis* 37 (4), pp. 147–8.

Korman, Daniel, forthcoming: The Language of The Ontology Room.

Lewis, David, and Lewis, Stephanie, 1970: Holes. In: *The Australasian Journal of Philosophy* 48, pp. 206–12.

Lowe, Jonathan, 2006: *The Four-Category Ontology.* Oxford: Oxford University Press.

Mally, Ernst, 1904: Untersuchungen zur Gegenstandstheorie des Messens. In: Meinong, Alexius (Hg.): *Untersuchungen zur Gegenstandstheorie und Psychologie* (Band 3). Leipzig: Barth, pp. 121–262.

McDaniel, Kris, 2010: Being and Almost Nothingness. In: *Nous* 4 (44), pp. 628–49.

McTaggart, John Ellis, 1908: The Unreality of Time. In: *Mind* 17, pp. 457–74.

Petersen, Thorben, in preparation: The Language of The Ontology Room.

Priest, Graham, 2005: *Towards Non-Being. The Logic and Metaphysics of Intentionality.* Oxford: Oxford University Press.

Putnam, Hilary, 1967: Time and Physical Geometry. In: *Journal of Philosophy* 64 (8), pp. 240–7.

Quine, Willard Van Orman, 1969: Speaking Of Objects. In: Quine, Willard Van Orman: *Ontological Relativity and Other Essays.* New York: Columbia University Press, pp. 1–25.

Recanati, François, 2004: *Literal Meaning.* Cambridge: Cambridge University Press.

Savitt, Steven, 2006: Presentism and Eternalism in Perspetive. In: Dieks, Dennis (ed.): *The Ontology of Spacetime.* Amsterdam: Elsevier, pp. 111–27.

Sider, Theodore, 1999: Presentism and Ontological Commitment. In: *Journal of Philosophy* 96 (7), pp. 325–47.

Sider, Theodore, 2009: Ontological Realism. In: Chalmers, David; Manley, David; Wasserman, Ryan (eds.): *Metametaphysics. New Essays on the Foundations of Ontology.* Oxford: Oxford University Press, pp. 384–423.

Turner, Jason, 2011: Ontological Nihilism. In: Bennett, Karen; Zimmerman, Dean (eds.): *Oxford Studies in Metaphysics Volume 6.* Oxford: Oxford University Press, pp. 3–54.

Wake, Andrew; Spencer, Joshua; and Fowler, Greogry, (2007): Holes as Regions of Spacetime. In: *The Monist* 3 (90), pp. 372-8.

Westerhoff, Jan, 2005: *Ontological Categories.* Oxford: Oxford University Press.

Williams, Clifford, 1996: The Metaphysics of A- and B-Time. In: *Philosophical Quarterly* 46 (184), pp. 471–81.

Verzeichnis der Autoren

Yuri Balashov
Department of Philosophy
107 Peabody Hall
The University of Georgia
Athens, GA 30602, USA
Phone: +1-706-583-0529
Fax: +1-706-542-2839
E-mail: yuri@uga.edu
Web page: http://yuri.myweb.uga.edu

Mauro Dorato
University of Rome 3,
Department of Philosophy
Via Ostiense, 234
00144 Rome, Italy
E-mail: dorato@uniroma3.it
Web page: http://host.uniroma3.it/dipartimenti/filosofia/personale/doratoweb.htm

Florian Fischer
Institut für Philosophie
Universität Bonn
Am Hof 1
53113 Bonn
E-mail: fischerf@uni-bonn.de
Web page: http://uni-bonn.academia.edu/FlorianFischer

Cord Friebe
Universität Bonn
Am Hof 1
53113 Bonn
E-mail: cfriebe@uni-bonn.de
Web page: http://www.philosophie.uni-bonn.de/personen/wissenschaftliche-mitarbeiter/pd-dr.-cord-friebe

Cody Gilmore
Department of Philosophy
University of California
One Shields Avenue
Davis, CA 95616-8673, USA
Skype: +1-530-554-4924
Fax: +1-530-752-8964
E-mail: gilmore@ucdavis.edu
Web page: http://sites.google.com/site/codysgilmore/

Thomas Müller
Janskerkhof 13a, kamer 1.10
3512 BL Utrecht, Netherlands
Tel.: +31-(0)30-2532097
Fax: +31-(0)30-2532816
E-mail: Thomas.Mueller@phil.uu.nl
Web page: http://www.phil.uu.nl/~tmueller

Thorben Petersen
Universität Bremen FB 9
Institut für Philosophie
Raum: SFG 4170
Enrique-Schmidt-Str. 7
28334 Bremen
Phone: +49-(0)421-218-67833
E-mail: tpetersen@uni-bremen.de
Web page: http://www.philosophie.uni-bremen.de/personen/wissenschaftliche-mitarbeiter.html?tx_jshuniversity_pi2[showUid]=653&cHash=8637ad1c58

PHILOSOPHIA NATURALIS

Eingereichte Beiträge dürfen weder schon veröffentlicht worden sein noch gleichzeitig einem anderen Organ angeboten werden. Mit der Annahme des Manuskriptes zur Veröffentlichung in der *Philosophia naturalis* räumt der Autor dem Verlag Vittorio Klostermann das zeitlich und inhaltlich unbeschränkte Nutzungsrecht im Rahmen der Print- und Online-Ausgabe der Zeitschrift ein. Dieses beinhaltet das Recht der Nutzung und Wiedergabe im In- und Ausland in körperlicher und unkörperlicher Form sowie die Befugnis, Dritten die Wiedergabe und Speicherung des Werkes zu gestatten. Der Autor behält jedoch das Recht, nach Ablauf eines Jahres anderen Verlagen eine einfache Abdruckgenehmigung zu erteilen.

Richtlinien zur Manuskriptgestaltung

Bitte jeden Beitrag mit *Titelblatt* abgeben, das folgende Angaben enthält: Name und Vorname des Autors / der Autorin (mit akad. Titel), Titel des Beitrags, vollständige Adresse (inkl. Telefon-Nummer), nähere Bezeichnung der Arbeitsstätte.

Die *Manuskripte* sollten 3-fach ausgedruckt und als Word- oder rtf-File eingereicht werden und ein deutsch- und englischsprachiges Abstract enthalten. Das Manuskript sollte einen breiten Rand haben.

Der *Umfang* (einschließlich Anmerkungen und Bibliografie) soll bei den Aufsätzen nicht mehr als 30 maschinengeschriebene Seiten (ca. 2.000 Anschläge, 2-zeilig) betragen.

Für *Abbildungen* im Text bitte die Originalvorlage einreichen. Abbildungen müssen numeriert und mit Autorennamen versehen sein.

Zitate im Text sollten vom Haupttext durch eine Leerzeile abgehoben werden. Nach dem zitierten Text stehen Name des zitierten Verfassers, Erscheinungsjahr und Seitenangaben in Klammern, z.B.: (Elkana 1974, S. 34). Bei mehreren Autoren werden die jeweiligen Namen durch Schrägstriche getrennt, z.B.: Krantz/Luce/Suppes/Tversky 1971, S. 8). Wird auf mehrere Publikationen desselben Autors im selben Erscheinungsjahr verwiesen, so sollen sie numeriert werden: (Ludwig 1970 a) bzw. (Ludwig 1970 b).

Die *Anmerkungen* sind im Manuskript fortlaufend zu numerieren; sie stehen am Schluss des Beitrags in numerischer Reihenfolge.

Für das anschließende *Literaturverzeichnis* in alphabetischer und chronologischer Reihenfolge gilt folgendes Muster:

Elkana, Y., 1974: *The Discovery of the Conservation of Energy*. London: Huchinson.

Clausius, R., 1850: Über die bewegende Kraft der Wärme. In: *Annalen der Physik und Chemie*, 79, S. 500–524.

Klein, M.J., 1978: The Early Papers of J. Willard Gibbs: A Transformation of Thermodynamics. In: E.G. Forbes (Hg.): *Human Implications of Scientific Advance*. Edinburgh: University Press, S. 330–341.

Korrekturen: Die Autoren erhalten vom Verlag die Fahnen ihres Beitrags mit der Bitte, die korrigierten Fahnen *innerhalb von zwei Wochen* an den Herausgeber zu schicken. In den Fahnen sollen nur noch Satzfehler berichtigt werden.

Nach Erscheinen des Heftes erhalten die Autoren 3 Belegexemplare des jeweiligen Heftes.

